Beyond the Beaten Paths: Driving Historic Galveston

JAN JOHNSON

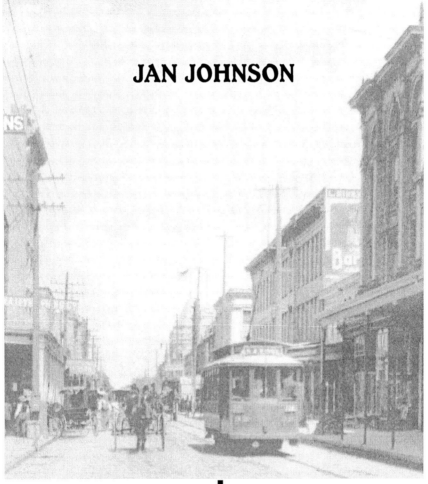

EAKIN PRESS ⫷ₑₚ⫸ Waco, Texas

Cover photo courtesy of the
Rosenberg Library, Galveston, Texas.

FIRST EDITION
Copyright © 2012 by Jan Johnson
Published in the United States of America
By Eakin Press—A Division of Sunbelt Media, Inc.
P.O. Box 21235 ᴁ Waco, Texas 76702
email: sales@eakinpress.com
💻 website: www.eakinpress.com 💻
ALL RIGHTS RESERVED.
1   2   3   4   5   6   7   8   9
ISBN 13: 978-1-935632-35-1
ISBN 10: 1-935632-35-3
Library of Congress Control Number 2012954068

Contents

Acknowledgments

The sequel to the city's first comprehensive walking guide, *Beyond the Beaten Paths: Driving Historic Galveston*, attempted to see all the sights and read the rest of the stories that the oldest city in Texas had to offer. With "more history per square inch" (according to Bob Nesbitt) than any other southern city, that challenge will require volumes and volumes; hence, my second offering!

To start at the beginning of the city's historical renaissance, I want to acknowledge the foresight of both the Kempner Fund and the Moody Foundation. In 1966-67 they funded John Garner and his Historic American Buildings Survey, which positioned our Island at the forefront of the historical preservation movement in the United States. In particular, a big thanks goes to the late Tim Thompson for hiring my mom, Dorris Stechmann Johnson, as Garner's secretary during that first year. Based on their research and interviews, the stories she told around the dinner table instilled my interest in my Island heritage at the young and impressionable age of thirteen.

My eternal gratitude must be given to the most patient staff of Rosenberg Library's Galveston–Texas History Center: Carol Wood, Mary Hernandez and Director Casey Greene, for their painstaking and on-going efforts to provide and protect all of its primary resources.

As before, I did not have to be an "Island unto Myself" in writing this book. My heartfelt "Thank you" to the cooperative community of caring friends, colleagues, most understanding employers, cheerleaders, and countless well-wishers, including friends Brenda Tortorice, Sally and Jim Laney, as well as Fay Allison, retired English teacher, who offered her own insight with heartfelt support.

I want to thank my understanding albeit less-than patient partner, Gene Bindhammer, who provided a pair of eyes and legs when none other were available, computer tech and motivator who supported me every step of the way (pun intended!).

Most of all, my sincere thankfulness goes to graphic designer Marshall Bayless, whose skills created ten multi-part, intricate maps of the island to accompany the text. No doubt they will prove an invaluable aid to my wandering readers, as the routes wind in and out of unfamiliar areas—not to mention Marshall's tenacity to keep me on track.

Grateful kudos to the many pairs of feet and eyes, who literally drove the routes and "walked the walks," to look over my shoulder with invaluable observations and suggestions: Jack and Cheryl Watson, Lynn Burke, Sherri Short, and Sigrun Burke, James Anderson, Sarah and Ken Jackson and, last but certainly not least, Carolyn Mytholar.

Many others gave generously of their time, first-hand experience and resources in the production of this driving guide. My heartfelt gratitude to all those learned writers and researchers who came before, whether paid professionals, architectural scholars, or passionate volunteers—bonded by our intrinsic and passionate love for Galveston Island and its history, whether BOIs or IBCs. Many of their names are listed in the Bibliography, but others deserve special recognition: Jane Chapin and Carlotta Barker again for all their work on so many neighborhood walking guides; Bill Cherry for sharing all of his precious memories of Galveston through his writings and videos; "THE Cemetery Lady" Linda McBee and husband, Doug; Elsie Badgett Graugnard for her memories of the quadruplets; FaceBook buddies Scott Fields, Frances Nussbaum, and BOI William "Bill" Pennington.

Those with specialized knowledge of Galveston's history include retired Rice professor, Jane Chance, now a proud "IBC;" the Galveston Island State Park staffers, Trey Goodman and Steve Alexander, especially for their introduction to Kirk Clark—his painstaking and passionate investigation of the old Nottingham Lace Factory was invaluable; the Jack and Welcome Wilson Jamaica Beach Museum via cousins Cindi Proler and Kathlene Wilson for providing vintage images of the development; and finally NOAA's Jo Anne Williams and Roger Zimmerman now headquartered in the restored Fort Crockett buildings for generously sharing its many historical documents and archives.

To all of my Osher Lifelong learners who took my class, "Discover Historic Galveston," who shared their stories and experiences, especially "Tiny" Walker, Retta Webber, Donna in La Marque, Lynn, Ollive, Betty, the Trittles, just to name a few, as well as Michelle Sierpina who allowed me to teach it! Another nod to a most generous James Anderson—all of whom proved that as a teacher I could be taught!

As with my first book, I relied primarily upon Beasley and Fox's *Galveston Architectural Guide*. Dedicated to Galveston Historical Foundation's quintessential Executive Director Peter Brink, this break-through book chronicled 234 pages worth of structures, divided into seven sections complete with photos and detailed maps. However, with its publication date of 1996, this guide has become sorely out-of-date and needs a more current update for future generations of passionate history buffs.

Since a simple "Thank You" is not enough, again I'd like to borrow a phrase from Shakespeare's *Twelfth Night* to gratefully acknowledge each and every one of you—

"Thanks and Thanks and EVER Thanks!!"

Introduction

For those of you who enjoyed walking the streets of historic Galveston, *Beyond the Beaten Paths: Driving Historic Galveston* travels most of the 32-mile length of the Island via often circuitous routes that meander in, out and around those nine distinct historical neighborhoods traversed in the city's first walking guide. Deeper in the districts, the wanderer will discover many few and far-between vintage structures, while reading more in-depth studies about many of the Island's lesser known but thoroughly unforgettable characters—however they achieved their place in its history. Along the way, one may notice various markers, plaques and monuments denoting a structure's or resident's historical significance, so this introduction will conclude with descriptions of their shape and explanations of the meanings of each.

Even more than the first, this guidebook is meant for the curious "Everyman" who travels city streets, avenues and roads, wondering about Galveston's past, rather 50 or 500 years ago. While the walking guide focused on those documented stories after the city was officially established by Michel Menard in 1839, the driving guide includes the Island's more mythic yarns, spanning its 500+ years of human habitation. That "ancient history" started as early as 1528 when Spanish sailor Cabaza de Vaca encountered the Karankawa Indians on his "Malhaldo." While we are fortunate that his story had been recorded, many more are buried in legend and lore. Despite a lack of concrete evidence, these tales are nevertheless worth telling and the sites are worth seeing. Beware the term "legend" in the text as it may signal one of those refutable "Tour Guide Tales"—perhaps undocumented but interesting and astoundingly good stories! Just accept and enjoy them as "folklore . . . in the oral tradition."

In addition, *Driving Historic Galveston* also includes narratives that originated within structures lost over time, only viewed via vintage images when available. By going beyond the concrete, wandering readers are encouraged to engage their imaginations for a deeper understanding into the city's past, to further appreciate the deep, rich heritage in both time and space.

As for "few-and-far-between," the term means exactly that— you may drive two or three blocks with only a couple of structures listed; however, you will pass many more whose inside stories simply remain unknown. Perhaps their rebirth through restoration will encourage their stories to be researched, told and/or publicly documented. Even if the inside stories of structures are unknown, they are certainly interesting and worth noting from the outside—and wondering about!

Oh, all the sites you'll see! Quite literally from one end of the Island to the other—almost. With an ambitious aim to include everything not covered in the first book, *Beyond the Beaten Paths* begins at the port to meander the vast residential east end with its elegant Victorian "painted ladies" that housed The Strand's most successful merchants. After a walk of the city's old "farmer's market," the reader will travel south of Broadway to discover the modest homes of the 19th century working class.

En route to visit Galveston's first cemetery, you'll wind your way westward through eclectic mid-town neighborhoods, to see more of its middle-class housing from the early 1930s forward to mid-20th-century "modern" residences. Following Avenue S as it slithers further west to become Stewart Road, history seekers will explore the city's airport located adjacent to modern attractions destination-designed for visitors . . . that provide a gateway to the Island's once rural and rustic West End. Two well-manicured golf courses and a contemporary country club lead to what's left of the once-lavish Stewart Mansion, private property now crumbling with age. Merging onto FM 3005, you will pass several early beach communities with structures ranging from expendable "camps" to new, multi-million dollar designer dream homes and high-rises.

Traveling back east via the Seawall, you'll pass the site of a legendary 1900 Storm tragedy to encounter the city's second-oldest cemetery. Completing your journey of historic Galveston from its second-oldest house to early-to-mid-20th century arts and crafts cottages, your foray into history will halt at the east end of the Seawall, staring out at the Gulf of Mexico as massive ships line up to enter or leave Galveston Bay on their way to or from the Houston Ship Channel.

Covering this much ground necessitates a mode of transportation other your feet; i.e., something with wheels—a car, bicycle, motorcycle, segway, carriage with horse and driver, skateboard, scooter . . . (you get the picture!) for going these long distances. Wheeled transport inevitably leads to traffic—so please stay safe on the city streets and avenues. It is strongly suggested that you read the text and study the routes before you take to those streets. How about making your journey into Galveston's past a collaborative venture—share with a friend or two to help safely navigate and share your adventure, rather than a solo approach?

As you drive, feel free to pull over to park and walk even a block or two for a more up close and personal view—definitely encouraged for safety's sake. Two walks are featured in chapters 3 and 5—the Postoffice Promenade and the Broadway Cemetery—as well as portions of several other select neighborhoods.

Remember that when you park and leave your vehicle to walk, make sure that you hide valuables out of sight, perhaps in a

Texas Historical Commission, 1417 Sealy Ave

3

trunk—and lock your car. Please respect the privacy and property of residents by staying on the public sidewalks, right-of-ways or curbs; toward that end, none of the current homeowners are named in the book. For your own safety while on foot, be aware of uneven sidewalks, caused by the old, unseen roots of large live oak trees, or none at all and watch your step!

As mentioned in the walking guide, please remember that the facts in any book, based on present knowledge, remains fluid over time as new information is researched, revealed, re-interpreted then accepted. The true mark of wisdom is the acknowledgment that one cannot know everything at any given time, but can and will continue searching, with humility and a passion for the truth. And this writer for one can certainly be taught! For periodic updates, check out **www.GalvestonIslandGal.com**.

Navigating the City

Before you take to the streets, take a moment to review the city's layout, itself a relic from the past, by looking at several of the various chapter maps. Notice the mostly checkerboard grid of the new city as developed by engineer John D. Groesbeck of Albany, New York. Picking up where Thomas Borden (see Chapter 8) left off, he fashioned a simple and logical pattern after Texas won her Independence from Mexico in 1836. Beginning in the east end on the port side, his city plat extended as far west as 57th Street.

Basically, the streets that run approximately north and south are numbered, while the east/west avenues are lettered. Broadway (or Avenue J, a name no one uses) bisects the city east and west halfway between the Port (or Bay) side and the beach (or Gulf of Mexico) side. Originally, Groesbeck designed 25th Street as the primary north/south street, connecting the central business district with bath houses along the Gulf of Mexico. Even numbered addresses are found on the north side of the street—the more prestigious side as it captured cooling southern breezes—with odd on the south throughout the city; likewise, on numbered streets, the even numbers are on the east side with odd on the west.

South of Broadway and west of 25th Street was considered rural since it was so far from the central business district. Groesbeck platted ten-acre outlots here, each consisting of four regular city blocks. These could either be settled as farms, dairies, plantations or extra large country estates for the wealthiest, to be subdivided as the city moved south and west.

As necessary, the outlots were cut through east to west as needed, creating "½ streets" which run parallel to their lettered avenues one block to the north. Since the widths of these new ½ avenues were not standardized, some of those avenues are more like one-car-wide alleys—only to become full-sized widths across the next street!

A more problematic puzzle was created as officials honored prominent city fathers by naming streets after them. To avoid further confusion, street signs should reflect both letter or number designation as well as its name. Two things that should also be acknowledged: over the 184 years, some of the addresses may have been altered a tad; also, some of the street signs may be missing— give the instructions your most logical guess!

About one-third of the Island's land, primarily west of 61st Street, sat outside Groesbeck's 1838 grid, wide open for random development. Therefore, the further west you travel, the more random the plat. As mid-20th century developers cut man-made channels, newer neighborhoods grew up around them and the regular checker board pattern disappeared into more modern, planned communities. This is particularly true once you head "Down the

Centennial Borden Monument, 39th and Ave P

Island" to the rustic West End with its multitudinous beach communities.

Navigating this Guide

To help avoid confusion, this book primarily refers to the streets as numbers (ignoring the names) and the avenues by name, if they have one. There are exceptions to this rule: 25th Street, the primary north/south thoroughfare, whose number designation is interchanged with Rosenberg Avenue, as well as Avenue P with Bernardo de Galvez and Tremont with 23rd. Beginning at the Causeway (aka Interstate 45 or I 45) at 59th Street and traveling east to Seawall Boulevard at 6th Street, Broadway equally splits the city north and south. Since the city began at its natural harbor on Galveston Bay, you will find the beginning letters on its port side and lower numbers on the east end of the Island.

City of Galveston Landmark Plaque, 1524 Avenue K

Traveling instructions are given in bold type, as are addresses. The numbers signal a change of driving/walking direction and correlate with the circled numbers on the maps, NOT structures of interest. In the cases of 2 or 3 turns in the instructions, the second is designated as b; the third, c. Maps are provided for every chapter, but it may be helpful to carry or refer to a compass at times.

Each chapter begins where the previous chapter ended. If planning your journey in a more random fashion, please understand that your beginning directions may alter a bit from how and where you choose to approach it.

Vicinities explored in *Beyond the Beaten Paths: Driving Historic Galveston* include:

- Chapter 1: "Driving Historic Harborside"—more than anything else, Galveston's natural harbor played a pivotal role in the city's success, even before it was officially founded.
- Chapter 2: "East on Postoffice, West on Church Avenues"—after a brief sojourn to see "Old Red" on the U.T.M.B. campus.
- Chapter 3: "Postoffice Promenade"—the guide's first designated walk.
- Chapter 4: "Galveston's Victorian East End."
  A. North of Broadway.
  B. . . . then South.
- Chapter 5: "Meandering Through Mid-town to Walk the Broadway Cemetery."
- Chapter 6: "The City Spreads West—to the Airport."
- Chapter 7: "Down the Island"—beyond the Seawall to Jamaica Beach.
- Chapter 8: ". . . And Back Again"—from 103rd to 25th Street (aka Rosenberg Avenue).
- Chapter 9: "All the Way East"—to the other end of the Island.

Many of these routes cross those major thoroughfares featured in *Walking Historic Galveston*. While brief descriptions of some historical sites are included in this guide, you will be referred to the first to find out more information about them. This guidebook uses such directional markers as: "to" or "on your right or left," "north or south," "east or west" side of the "street or avenue."

Distinctive Plaques

As you drive and/or walk around Galveston's out-of-the-way areas, you may notice various markers, monuments or plaques either on porches or freestanding in yards. While many of them were awarded by the state-directed agencies over the years, those much more evident are prominently displayed next to the homes' front doors. These originated with Island entities and each has its own significance. An explanation of those with official recognition follows, even though several homeowners have elected to erect their own less-uniform private plaques.

Centennial Markers

To celebrate the Republic of Texas Centennial in 1936, the Texas Legislature appropriated $3 million and created the Commission for Control to supervise the statewide celebrations. In addition to the staging of pageants and an industrial exposition chronicling the state's progress, many monuments, memorials and grave markers were erected to recognize early patriots and historic places. A total

GHF 1900 Storm Survivor and East End Historical District Christmas Tour

8

of 1,100 such markers were installed around the state, including large, granite-based monuments sporting the state's seal. Galveston Island definitely has its fair share of these, including a Jean Lafitte marker on old Stewart Road and one fronting 39th Street of the Thomas Henry Borden home on Avenue P (aka Bernardo de Galvez Avenue).

Texas Historical Commission State Markers

The purpose of this governmental organization, created in 1953, was to recognize and celebrate this state's unique history and preservation. In addition to being made caretakers of the 1936 granite markers, the THC is responsible for awarding plaques for a Recorded Texas Historic Landmark, National Register of Historic Places, State Archeological Landmarks and the more recent Historic Texas Cemetery. To receive this recognition, an extensive application process with complete documentation must be submitted to prove a location's historical significance. If judged deserving, the Commission presents a bronze plaque with its seal, and specific instructions as to its installation. At present, there are 15,000 throughout the state and ALL are listed on the Texas Historic Sites Atlas at www.thc.state.tx.us.

City of Galveston Landmark Designation

In March, 1999, the City Council passed an ordinance to signify those specific structures already recognized from off the Island that "demonstrate distinctive characteristics or association with significant people or events on the Island." Among those listed in this book are the Texas Building at 22nd and Postoffice, the 1839 Samuel May Williams home at 36th and Avenue P, and 1524 Avenue K, pictured on page 6.

Galveston Historical Foundation Plaques

This non-profit organization that serves as custodian of historical presentation offers a variety of plaques to homeowners.

The oval bronze markers that you see next to the front doors of historic houses are given to those owners who have opened their private residences during the GHF's annual Historic Homes Tour, held during the first two weekends in May—one for every year the house participated. You may note multiple plaques on one residence.

Homeowners can purchase the diamond-shaped plaques with a line reading "1900 Storm Survivor," by making application to the Foundation. Once GHF has authenticated the year of construction, the plaque is awarded.

A slender rectangle with a horizontal blue arrow denotes the "Ike Waterline" with the date, September 13, 2008. This demonstrates the depth of the toxic water at that location during that most destructive storm, usually to celebrate the home's salvation and/or restoration.

The East End Historic District

Their vertical rectangular marker signifies that the house was opened to the public during the association's annual Christmas Tour of Homes. This event happens only the Friday night before Dickens on The Strand from 6-10 PM, featuring a limited number of structures and no more than 220 tickets offered for sale.

GHF Ike Waterline, 1st and Postoffice

Before you take to your car to explore the streets and avenues of the Island city, please take the time to read the text and study the routes from the comfort of your armchair before venturing out in traffic. Then, discover the many overlooked historic sites, although far-between, however you want, following your journey according to your whims: break the routes into more manageable lengths, walk blocks, stop for lunch along the way, photograph houses, dig deeper into the cemeteries (figuratively speaking . . .), linger longer, and let your imagination wander—whatever! Just get started—full of colorful stories and characters, Galveston's few and far-between sites, off-the-beaten paths await you wandering readers!

As in *Walking Historic Galveston*, this driving guidebook begins portside on the street lining its natural harbor.

Behind resident dog, Lewis' wood carving, note the Home's Tour and 1900 Storm Survivor plaques from GHF and the East End's Christmas Tour, 13th and Sealy

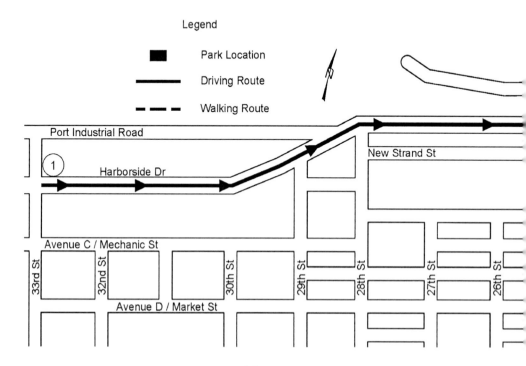

CHAPTER 1

Driving Historic Harborside

Originally known as Avenue A or Water on the 1838 Groesbeck city grid, the street next to the natural harbor on Galveston Bay was renamed Port Industrial in 1964 in recognition of the city's marine and manufacturing industries. As the waterfront developed

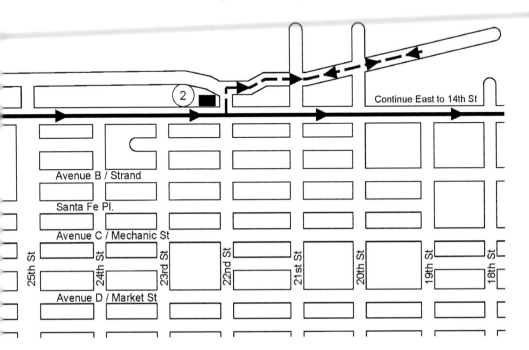

into a tourist destination beginning with the addition of *Elissa* in 1979, the name was changed to Harborside Drive.

▶ ❶ **Start your leisurely drive at 33rd Street, travelling east.**

The Grain Elevators

In 1839, the first wharf to be built on the natural port stood at the foot of 29th Street, replaced by the first immigration station fourteen years later. Although cotton was still king until the 1970s, Galveston built its first grain elevator during the 1890s to become a leading grain exporting port. Elevator B with its six-million bushel capacity followed in 1930 at this location and the island city led the nation in grain exports by 1951. With times ever changing, the old 236-foot high complex was imploded in 10 seconds at 7 A.M. on September 16, 2003, to make way for an expanded second cruise ship terminal to accommodate Royal Caribbean.

Piers 23-26

Built in 1927 for the Mallory Line, this warehouse stored incoming cargo and cotton. To meld into the urban landscape of Rosenberg Avenue (aka 25th Street), the simple concrete build-

Mallory Dock

—From the author's collection

ing featured a centered two-storied bay inset with arches. In 1990, the Rapp Brothers converted it into a passenger terminal which would not be used on a regular basis until September, 2000, when Carnival Cruise Lines sailed into Galveston. Offering cruises to the Caribbean year-round on the *Celebration*, they doubled their sailings within five years and built an expanded parking area and motor coach staging area. The Texas homeport celebrated its current sixth-place ranking in the cruise ship industry by luring the brand new Carnival *Magic* with Disney and Princess cruises in port's future.

Across the Bay you will see Pelican Island, which has become the industrial side of the harbor. Note the many oil rigs and platforms being repaired. If you're lucky, you might see one being piloted out of the port to return to its exploration duties in the Gulf of Mexico.

2311-2313 Harborside Drive
Originally, the 1876 Butterowe buildings, used as a corn and oats warehouse, fronted Avenue A; hence their odd-numbered addresses. Gus A. Butterowe, Jr., employed them to house his sheet metal business, adding the west annex during the 1940s. Today, these two-story buildings have been converted into lofts, overlooking the port. Their southern side, overlooking The Strand, has recently been modified into dramatic ghost/pirate attractions. On the corner of Tremont (aka 23rd Street) and Strand stands the 1916 Armour and Company building (see *Walking Historic Galveston: A Guide to its Neighborhoods*).

▶ ❷ **Turn left off Harborside at 22nd Street.**

Park in one of the parking lots and walk the next three blocks for a closer view. Before, during or after, have a bite to eat at one of the harbor-view restaurants, but confirm first that a validated ticket will give you three hours of free parking.

▶ **Walk to the right to see or perhaps visit the Texas Seaport Museum. Continue walking east to the right.**

The *Elissa*

To celebrate the city's maritime successes, the Galveston Historical Foundation searched for and found an original 19th century sailing ship in Greece. Although she was in a much altered state, a brass plaque on her main mast authenticated this three-masted, iron hulled barque as *Elissa*, #294 built by Alexander Hall and Co. of Aberdeen, Scotland in 1877. Research revealed that she had actually called at the port of Galveston twice: on December 26, 1883, with a cargo of bananas from Tampico, Mexico and again three years later. Purchased for $40,000 in 1975, her hull was repaired where she was found enabling the *Elissa* to be towed to her new home on July 20, 1979. Her $4 million restoration complete by 1982, she opened for tours on July 4, marking the area's beginning transformation from industrial to visitor-friendly. That Labor Day she sailed again under full 19 sails—her first in over 50 years. The *Elissa* is one of the only square-rigged tall ships in the world that has sailed in three centuries, meaning that her volunteer crew can experience 19th century sailing in 21st century waters.

Notice the figurehead on the ship's bow. While the face was based on a photo of a young Mary Moody (Northen), the artist was having difficulty getting perspective on the body. To solve the problem, a Texas A&M coed maritime student was actually strapped to *Elissa*'s bow one morning, suspended over the water, while the artist sketched and/or sculpted on the dock — this according to several volunteers.

The barque is docked at the Texas Seaport Museum. Inside and upstairs, you will find a user-friendly immigration database of ships' logs that list an estimated 200,000 passengers who came to America through the Port of Galveston between 1835 and 1935. Included in the pertinent information are countries of origin as well as departure and arrival dates, names, ages, gender, occupations. Truly, a genealogist's dream!

The museum also hosts the Pier 21 Theatre, which shows three short documentaries: "The Great (1900) Storm," one on the pirate Jean Lafitte, and a recent addition, "Galveston: Gateway to the Gulf."

The Texas Star Flour Mill stood on the block between 20th and 22nd streets on Avenue A from 1879 until 1972 when it was torn down. Founded by Czech brothers, John and Gustav Reymershoffer, the successful grain and rice mill cultivated trade with the West Indies, Mexico and Central America. Although the family sold its interests in 1904, the mill continued in operation until 1957.

Texas Star Flour Mill, 20th-22nd and Harborside
—Courtesy of The Rosenberg Library, Galveston, Texas

▶ **Continue walking east.**

The Mosquito Fleet

In addition to transport vessels, the Port of Galveston berthed various fishing boats throughout its history. Among the most recognizable were the shrimp boats docked at Pier 19. They are commonly called the "Mosquito Fleet" because their trawling nets resembled the outspread wings of the blood-sucking insects. The shrimp industry attracted commercial fishermen from all over the world—Italy, Greece, the West Indies, Europe and Scandinavia, even Cajuns from Louisiana Bayous—passing the tradition forward for two to five generations. To honor Galveston's place in such a successful business, a wooden shrimp boat christened in 1937 was donated by owners Joe and Edna Grillo to GHF's Texas Seaport Museum in 2002. You'll still find her berthed at Pier 19, slip 9B. Recently, shrimpers from Vietnam and other Asian countries have joined the fleet, which has been blessed for many springs by Catholic, Orthodox, and Episcopal priests.

Also docked in this area are several companies offering regular tours of Galveston's natural harbor, including the non-profit Galveston Historic Foundation.

Ocean Star

The retired jack-up drilling rig moored alongside the Mosquito Fleet houses the Offshore Energy Center. Open seven days a week, this museum features three floors of models, exhibits, videos and interactive displays using real equipment to inform visitors about today's offshore oil industry, paying homage to its early pioneers, its technological yet environmentally attuned advancements and vast underwater energy reserves.

▶ **Retrace your steps back to your car. Turn left on Harborside Drive to resume your easterly drive.**

Note the 1910 Galveston Ice and Cold Storage on the corner of 21st and Harborside, with its smokestack behind. You'll find more information about it in the walking guide.

Lipton Tea Building

At 19th and Harborside Drive stands the old Lipton Tea plant. Construction started on this $705,000 five-story plant on January 18, 1950, after the company "selected Galveston in view of the advantageous offer" which included overnight female companionship, according to some sources.

Mary Russell, a good friend of Mayor Herbert Cartwright, recruited well-bred college coeds to work at her bordello during the summer. After his Honor discovered the Lipton Tea scouting executive had a weakness for beautiful, young Christian women well-bred and mannered, the madam imported a stunning 19-year-old Dallas courtesan with "manners so impeccable she could have had tea with the Queen of England." In her company, Cartwright traveled to Lipton's New York offices several times which enticed the exec to visit the Island. Arriving at the scout's Hotel Galvez suite early one weekend morning with contract in hand, Mayor Herbie quickly secured his signature before his new lady friend returned "from teaching her Sunday school class."

The grand opening of Lipton Tea's Galveston plant on March 1, 1951, featured a tour of the new facilities to demonstrate how raw tea imported from Ceylon, India, China, Indonesia, Japan and Africa would be blended and processed on the Island for at least the next 25 years. Toward the end of its operation, spiced teas were produced; when demand dropped off, the plant officially closed on March 26, 1991.

▶ **Continue driving east.**

1700 The Strand

William Lawrence Bottomley of New York originally designed this three-story building as an immigration station in 1933 but, with demand decreasing, it became a U.S. Customs office in 1940. Spanish Baroque Revival in style, it features twin wings to its north that form a courtyard facing Harborside Drive. Declared surplus in 1976, the University of Texas Medical Branch housed their technology department and educational outreach programs here until the murky salt waters of Hurricane Ike damaged much of the original masonry. With a $10 million grant from the Economic Development Administration, the old customs house will be renovated and restored as an "adaptive reuse" combining historic preservation with modern "green" technology.

1417 Harborside

Between 15th and 14th streets, you will pass the site of buccaneer Jean Lafitte's house. Angered by the Louisiana governor's refusal to acknowledge him as a hero in the Battle of New Orleans, he sailed west to the island of "Galvez Town" in 1816. He commandeered the deserted French colony of Louis d'Aury to establish his own pirate colony, called Campeche. Flying the Mexican flag with letters of marquee from Columbia, Lafitte established himself as its corsair CEO, earning the title, "Terror of the Gulf." He built a wood-frame house/fort on this site, naming it Maison Rouge after its bright red color, and furnished it with the best pirate booty pilfered by his hired "freebooters." Armed with two cannons on the second floor aimed at the bay to protect his flagship, the *Jupiter*, his fort home also featured a wine cellar—everything befitting a pirate king! Forced to leave Galveston in 1820, he burned his settlement to the ground. During the 1870s, another house was built here based on Lafitte's original Maison Rouge design. The damaged foundations still exist, built over his wine cellar—now privately-owned property. (For more information on Lafitte, see Chapter 7— "Down the Island.")

Your drive down historic Harborside is now complete.

CHAPTER 2

East on Postoffice, West on Church Avenues

▶ ❶ From Harborside, turn right on 13th Street. Turn left on The Strand and onto the campus of the University of Texas Medical Branch. Continue driving east until you reach a roundabout.

902-928 Strand

Following the turn-around, you'll note the 1890 Asbel Smith Building dwarfed by several newer and much taller buildings. Designed by Nicholas J. Clayton, this Romanesque Revival wears masonry of Texas sandstone, red pressed brick and granite, giving it a distinct rosy hue and the nickname, "Old Red." Slated for demolition in UTMB's 1965 Master Plan, it was allowed to deteriorate, becoming home to pigeons—living, dead and dying. The Galveston Historical Foundation, alumni and faculty saved it in 1983. Its privately-funded restoration was completed three years later.

▶ ❷ Retrace your route back to 13th Street and turn left.

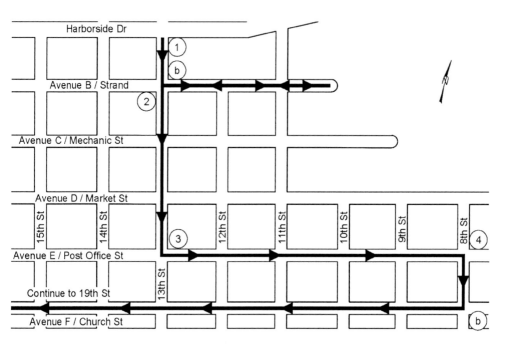

Crossing Market, you will pass the Rosenberg, Runge and Reymershoffer homes on the right, all of which are listed in the walking guide.

▶ ❸ Turn left on the east-bound one-way street Avenue E

Avenue E was renamed Postoffice because the U.S. Custom house at the corner of 20th Street originally housed the city's Post Office (see *Walking Historic Galveston*).

416 13th Street

This home, built in 1880 by Gustav Heye, fronts 13th Street with a long veranda to catch the southeastern breezes off the Gulf. A commission merchant and cotton factor, Heye served as a blockade runner during the Civil War.

1212 Postoffice Avenue

Built by printer Louis Blaylock in 1873, this five-bay-wide home featured double doors centered beneath twin dormers.

1207 Postoffice

On the south side of the street stands the Davidson/Penland house. A stand-out among other East End cottages, the late Greek Revival one-story cottage was built between 1866-68 of cypress and long-leaf pine. Marked by four columns with a transom framing its front door, the home also features a hip-roof.

One of city's first founding fathers, Norwegian pilot boat Captain John Davidson bought this lot from Rufus Cage for $500 on August 22, 1866, and a house stood here two years later. Despite a lawsuit by the heirs of Dennis Campion who challenged his ownership two years later and were awarded extra fees, Davidson retained this house, one of four belonging to him on the avenue. On Sunday, December 13, 1868, the captain died a hero trying to rescue the pilot of the bark, *Fortuna*, which was ferrying immigrants from Breman, Germany. Two years later, his widow Sophia sold the house to Byron and Mary McKeen. She was the daughter of Henry Francis Fisher, who had led the way for German immigration to Texas. Financial difficulties necessitated the sale of the home to Samuel Moore Penland at public auction at a loss on September 14, 1872. This great nephew of Sam Houston sold the property ten years later, but stayed on the Island, active in the community until his death on February 10, 1922. The house contin-

1207 Postoffice

ued to change hands numerous times over the years, and even served as the parson's residence for the First Presbyterian Church from 1882-1893.

In 2011 the current owner, through her meticulous research, secured recognition for the home by the Texas Historic Commission, as well as that of the City of Galveston. The designation reads the home's owners and their ancestors contributed "significant(ly) to the history of Galveston and . . . the State's earliest history."

1202 Postoffice—Purity Ice Cream

Bakers Gustav and Emil Kahn arrived from Germany in 1888 to establish a confectionary shop two years later at 2107 Market. Built circa 1878, this structure housed an ice cream parlor and factory owned by Benjamin F. Willis and partner Jerrie J. Sullivan. By 1914 the Kahn brothers had moved their shop to this location, doubling its size by 1931. Ice cream was still produced here as late as 1990, after which Lt. Blender started producing cocktail mixes in a bag.

Purity Ice Cream, 12th and Postoffice
—Courtesy of The Rosenberg Library, Galveston, Texas

1127 Postoffice

Atypical of most two-story corner grocery stores on the Island, this A&P Tea Company building incorporates late Craftsman design within its 1931 high raised wood bungalow. Note its casement windows, outside stairway and second floor front porch.

1128 Postoffice

Doctor, chemist and apothecary H.C.L. Aschoff started building this gabled Southern townhouse with double galleries in 1859, but his family home was not completed until after the Civil War.

1122, 1118, and 1114 Postoffice—"Three Sisters' Houses"

These three two-story homes were built for the Aschoff daughters circa 1888.

1115 Postoffice

In 1962, Galveston architect Louis Oliver modernized this 1932 bungalow with a screened façade and freestanding garage.

1112 Postoffice

Built around 1865, this house was moved here from the Sabine Pass by barge after the 1900 Storm.

914 Postoffice

This home was originally built two blocks east on the north side of the street by Frederich Wagenbredt circa 1879. He owned a coffee stand in the 900 block of The Strand. Three years after his widow died in 1905, a home-based candy maker named Henry Werner bought the cottage, moving it to this Postoffice location in June 1924. At that time, a larger addition, perhaps in front, doubled its size. Although it resembles Greek Revival, its small front gable with a flat roof belies that style. Twenty-one years later, Laura V. Werner sold it to fisherman Mauro Patane and his wife Josephine.

▶ ❹ Continue driving one block east to 8th Street, where you will turn right. Turn right again onto Church Avenue, a one-way street travelling west.

Avenue F was appropriately named Church for the number of religious sanctuaries located along it. On the south side of the street in this block, notice the group of Gulf Coast cottages, most built in 1892.

809, 811, 813, and 815 Church

Brick contractor Benjamin F. Barnes built four identical tenant homes as rentals on the south side of the street. Over the years, their original floor plans have been altered. The cottage at **809** was lengthened to add a side entrance complete with small porch on its east side, while the 1895 Victorian at **815** had a second floor added during the 1890s, making it a two-story shotgun house with a double gallery.

806 and 810 Church

On the north side of the street, real estate investor Henry M. Trueheart bought these three lots to build two gabled Victorian cottages in 1882. Before that sale, three African Americans rented the lots and were forced to move the houses they had built to other locations.

818 Church

Also built by Barnes at another location, this five-bay-wide, dormered 1885 Creole cottage featured a central hall separating two rooms on either side. The current homeowner, John, discovered a family connection with this home while researching his Island roots. It seems that during the Great Storm of 1900, neighbor Captain Harris rescued his then six-month-old father from this house by holding the infant high overhead while wading through water. John corresponded with the owner from 1959 until her death in 1985; during that time, she determined that the house should belong to him! Feeling that it was "meant to be," he and his wife bought it around the turn of the 21st century; it was featured as a "Restoration in Progress" during the 2002 Galveston Historic Homes Tour.

824 Church

Brick contractor Benjamin also built this deeper-set five-bay cottage with its low-pitched roof and smaller rear wing.

828 Church

Occupying the property as early as 1872, Barnes chose the northwest corner of 8th and Church for his own family. This raised Gulf Coast cottage with its hipped roof was not built, however, until 1883.

903 Church Avenue on the southwest corner

Construction date and original location was unknown on this Gulf Coast cottage but insurance records indicate that it was moved to this site in 1931.

907 Church

Marble contractor John Quick built this five-bay cottage in 1867.

915 Church

Built in 1881 as a simple one story cottage by William H. Reid, this Greek Revival design sold to Captain William Wallace

818 Church

Woolford and his wife Oneida ten years later. Of old English ancestry, the captain commanded the U.S. tug boat, *Anna*, while his wife raised two children. By 1914, the size of the house had doubled to 5,072 square feet when the first floor was raised and a new ground level constructed beneath. Unmarried daughter Ida Belle continued to live in the home until her death in 1982 at age 97.

923 Church

Especially note the front door within the third bay of this four-bay tenant home. Insurance records indicate that it was built for Miss Kate Rogers in 1901 perhaps of salvaged material from 1900 Storm damage.

926 Church

Arthur B. Homer, the youngest brother of famous 19th century American painter Winslow, remodeled this large house in 1883 for himself and Alice Patch. Note in particular its triple high-pitched gambrel roof, three arched veranda bays, and brick-like shingles. Behind the Homer home stood the original carriage house for the next entry.

523 10th Street

Across the street, insurance agent Robert J. Hughes faced his imposing 1874 Italianate Villa to the east to catch the Gulf's southern breezes. With its stables next door, the house was expanded three times over the years adding a ballroom and a bay window along Church Avenue. Having served as the Russian consulate, a fraternity home and boarding house, the villa is currently being restored as a Bed and Breakfast.

1015 Church

Co-owner of the original Star Drug Store, Gaston H. Wilder built this 1902 raised cottage with its small front porch flanked by double windows.

1016 Church

This stately red brick house was built by stevedore company president Richard P. Williamson in 1926. Note the porta cache on its west side—a distinctive contrast in this East End neighborhood! The current homeowners recently funded the large tree carving of a bouquet of flowers in a shell vase.

1016 Church

526 11th Street

Although part of the house is located on the northeast corner on Church, dentist Dr. William S. Carruthers fronted his double-veranda, two-story home on 11th Street to better catch the southern Gulf breezes—similar to the more ornate Hughes house one block to its east.

▶ **Cross 11th Street.**

1107 Church Avenue

Standing behind a concrete parapet, this simple cottage, with its small porch centered below two windows, was built "on spec" in 1873 by carpenter Thomas Cordray. Mr. and Mrs. William Wood bought it upon completion, selling it to Dennis and Frances Fitzwilliam three years later. After they moved on in 1883, it became rental property, changing owners often. Even the unofficial "Lord of the Avenue" James S. Waters added it to his collection of houses on Church in 1902. The cottage did not find a permanent owner/resident until 1950 when UTMB secretary John Nolan moved in with his seamstress wife, Lillian. She lived here until her death in 1987.

1116 Church

"Lord" Waters built this large clapboard Victorian in 1893. After the neighboring house was torn down, this County treasurer and officer of several investment companies bought the corner lot four years later and added a gabled east bay with curved balcony and expansive garden. In 1902, Waters built the raised cottage at **1117 Church**, which resembles the Wilder home at 1015.

1124 Church

This one-and-one-half story, pointed gabled cottage was built by Mrs. Mary Cameron in 1892, just a year after her son, merchandise broker Allen E., built the large two-story Victorian next door. Note its pointed gable and decorative gingerbread.

1126-1128 Church

At the corner, note the unique roof line of Cameron's double-galleried house crowned by a widow's walk, intricate gingerbread, and the "Texas Star" within its front gable.

1127 Church

The decorative raised cottage on the south side of the street features a Gothic pointed arch in its gallery trim. Lawyer Charles L. Cleveland built it in 1877.

▶ Continue driving west on Church.

1211 Church (3rd from the corner to your left)

Shipsmith-turned-blacksmith Alexander B. Everett built this home in 1873. He continued to expand it as his family grew to eight children, creating a "stepped plan." Trimmed with unusual Victorian Rococo, its slender gabled entrance sits next to a front window bay, converting its style to an Italianate villa. Note another rear addition to the east. Sitting behind an iron fence with a carriage step inscribed "Everett," the house stayed in the family until 1982—more than 100 years!

1211 Church

1217 Church

Next door to the Everett home stands the Dealey residence, as noted on its carriage step. British-born Thomas W. Dealey immigrated to Galveston in August, 1870, and started working for the *Galveston News* as an office boy within the month. He married local girl Jennie Steele Howard in 1877, and built her this house two years later. The design of the house combined Louisiana's Creole with Greek Revival—front and back porches inset under the main roof with columns and a center hall floor plan. Thomas eventually ran Colonel Belo's Island newspaper while his brother, George, moved to Dallas to manage its sister paper; Dealey Plaza is named after this branch of the family. Active in the foundation of orphanages here, Thomas' deteriorating health moved the family to Mineral Wells, Texas, where he died in 1906.

1217 Church

1228 Church

This house is one of the few pre-Civil War houses in the city and one of the oldest in the district! In 1856, working class Joseph Ricke bought this lot from the Galveston City Company and built this classic three-bay revival-style cottage the following year. A separate kitchen was attached to the home by 1889. After he died in 1899, his widow Carolyn sold it to Louis Best on the condition that his family would take care of her until her death—which didn't happen until 1915. The house remained in the Best family until 1976—over 100 years of ownership by two families.

1311 Church

Moved to this location during the 1980s, this single story Gulf Coast cottage was originally built during the 1870s but where remains a mystery.

1323 Church

Nicholas J. Clayton designed this three-bay, two-story Southern townhouse in 1867 for drayman Ferdinand Miler. By the 1880s midwife Barbara L. Jacobs, who is credited with delivering more than 2,000 early "BOI" children, had moved here.

1401 Church

With its two bay windows fronting Church, this 1856 corner store housed William Werner's market. One of the oldest surviving corner stores on the Island, note its raised extension along 14th Street to catch the Gulf breeze.

1402 Church

Across the street, note the 1905 cottage. It was originally built by Herman B. Koppert as one of two tenant houses at 902 30th Street. His son sold the twin cottages to St. John's Missionary Baptist Church in 1972, and, twenty years later, the church donated both to the Galveston Historical Foundation. They moved one of them to this site and restored it using salvaged materials from the other; it sold in 1995. You'll find more information about the Koppert family in the walking guide.

1409 Church

Carpenter Henry Gardner built this tiny cottage, third from the corner, around 1869.

1428 Church

1428 Church

A native of South Windsor, Maine, seafarer Rufus Jameson settled in Galveston in 1853 to become a harbor pilot. Three years later, he bought these lots and built a smaller house for his wife, Sarah. During the Civil War, he tried to run the Union blockade but was imprisoned for three years, regularly writing letters home. Released, he returned to build a larger house for both his wife and newly-adopted daughter next door at **1420 Church** circa 1874. The present double-galleried corner home was completed in 1882. Unfortunately, Jameson lived here for less than a year, for he fell ill onboard the pilot boat *Eclipse* and died before reaching home. His widow Sarah lived here until her death in 1905 when the house passed to her granddaughter, Sara Woltson and husband Clint. It was vacant and deteriorating when the G.H.F. bought it in 1991 at a tax foreclosure sale. The current owners bought it in 2005 and restored it, then had to repair the Hurricane Ike-damaged first floor three years later. Note the large tree carving of a voluptuous mermaid holding a seashell.

519 15th Street

On this site sat the J. L. Darragh home, designed and built by Alfred Muller in 1887-8. After it lost its roof during a fire in December 1985, the Galveston Historical Foundation bought it, determined to restore it through many "Darragh Dinners" provided and funded by generous volunteers. By 1989, it sported a new roof, candle-snuffer turret and front galleries. Featured on the Historic Homes Tour, it sold in August 1990. Unfortunately, on the eve of restoration, three suspected arson fires in November caused its demolition the following year, leaving only the original 1889 cast-iron fence, also designed by Muller.

Irish businessman, John L. Darragh arrived on Galveston Island in March 1839. Within the year, he was elected Justice of the Peace and acquired the title of Judge, which would follow him throughout his life. An early city father and partner in the Galveston City Company, he became president of the Galveston Wharf Company in 1865. After the Civil War, he suffered a mental and physical decline and his first wife of 37 years divorced him in 1878. He quickly married Susan Earl, who died in childbirth two years later. Octogenarian Darragh married 50-years younger Laura Leonard in June 1881. With her husband suffering from dementia and declared legally insane, she supervised the construction of the house while caring for her two young sons, her stepson, and pregnant with her third child. After her husband died in Massachusetts in 1892, she continued to live here with her three sons until 1905, when it was leased as a boarding house. The Darragh descendents sold it in 1921.

In 1998, the East End Historic District converted the property into a neighborhood park, thanks to the generosity of E. Burke Evans. Ten years later, an iron pergola designed by Doug McLean provided the park's centerpiece in his honor. After Hurricane Ike's damage was restored, the Darragh Park was rededicated on April 17, 2009.

1510 Church

During Darragh's decline, he built three identical houses as rental property on the south side of 19th and Postoffice. In 1992, the American National Insurance Company purchased them to build a parking lot. Although they demolished two, Moody's insurance company donated the third to GHF, which moved it to this location. Due to Ike's toxic storm surge, Darragh's tenant house has been bought and restored twice.

1503 Church

Paul and Veska Chushcoff built this one-story, raised cottage fronting Church as rental property in December 1928. Calling it home over the years was a multicultural diverse economic group. A "tear-down" in 2002, the current owner re-oriented the entrance to 15th Street and incorporated the basement as living space to create an Island retreat overlooking the rose garden at Darragh Park.

1511 Church

This mid-19th century working class cottage was probably moved to this site from another. Its earliest title dates from 1879 when E. E. Steger bought it only to sell it two years later to Judge J. L Darragh. In 1938, Ira Miller purchased the house which remained in the family until 2002 when the Galveston Historical Foundation rescued and rehabilitated it either to be sold or leased.

The gabled cottage at **1520 Church** was built in 1894. You will find information about both **1602** and **1609 Church** in the walking guide.

▶ **Cross 16th Street.**

1706 and 1702 Church

1718 Church

1618 Church

Although little is known about most of the houses on this block, they are still worth noting as you drive to the sixth house to the right. The Great Fire of 1885 destroyed 40 square blocks of the west side of the East End Historic District overnight on Friday, November 13; this house replaced one of them. Determined not to lose another house to fire, owner Mrs. Rosa Peete insisted that her new home be constructed of brick and slate. Note its unusual mansard roof.

1627 Church

Walking Historic Galveston reported that saloon proprietor Edward A. Colleraine built this Clayton Southern townhouse in 1908. You will find more information about the other homes at this intersection in the walking guide.

1702 Church

Galveston's first female real estate developer, Mrs. Maud Moller built this Queen Anne Victorian as rental property in 1895, while her husband Jens worked as a ship broker. Other houses that she built include the house next door at **1706**, one around the corner at **513 17th Street**, two on **19th Street** as well as the family's residence at **1814 Sealy**.

1712 Church

Rebecca Ralston operated a boarding house at this address. Many working-class men and women were in need of temporary housing on the Island which created a market for one of the few acceptable opportunities for women—boarding house manager. Of the 175 operating in the city, 154 were owned by women in 1900.

1718 Church

On the preferable north side of the street, dry goods merchant Nephtali Grumback built a more substantial Victorian home in 1886, which conformed to the basic Galveston style: raised off ground level with high ceilings and wrap-around porches sporting walk-through windows. Note its centered open gable and double galleries, perhaps part of the 1906 remodeling done by C. W. Bulger.

1717 Church

Across the street you'll find this five-bay-wide raised cottage sporting a singular front porch, built in 1887 for Mrs. Emma Meyer.

1721 Church

Charles C. Allen of Alton, Illinois, came to Galveston around 1867 to supervise the building of the Galveston, Houston and Henderson Railroad Bridge, linking the island to the mainland. Although he still maintained his connection to Texas railroads, he also served as assistant postmaster and on city council. During Reconstruction under Governor Edmund J. Davis, he was the state senate secretary. When he died of gangrene in 1897, plans were already underway to build two wood-framed houses for his widow and son, both designed by George B. Stowe and within one block of each other. Callie Allen lived at **1819 Church** (which is no longer standing) until 1897, when she moved into this Queen Anne home with her son Charles, a storekeeper and stenographer for the Galveston City Railroad Company. In 1905, they sold it to J. W. Ravlin, who operated it as a boarding house. After his death in 1910, his widow Delia and daughter, Estelle continued to live here.

1722 Church

Born in Bremen, Germany, William Meininger moved his family to Galveston by 1884, to establish a wholesale produce business. Nine years later, he'd found his true calling as a wine merchant and commissioned a young George B. Stowe to build this transition home in 1896. Combining the earlier Queen Anne style with Colonial Revival details, the house pays homage to its owner's profession in the stained glass window over the stairway landing—a cupbearer pouring from a jug for Bacchus, the Greek god of wine—an interesting feature although not visible from the street. After Meininger died of a heart attack on July 6, 1904, the house eventually passed to his middle son, Julius. Sold in 1911 and divided into apartments, it was converted back into a single family residence in 1981. Over ten years later, the home was restored again, closer to its original Stowe design.

1728 Church

The Emanuel Bonart family lived above their dry goods shop on

Market between 25th and 26th Streets. He died in 1896, leaving his widow, Bertha, this simple Queen Anne/Craftsman home which was only half-constructed but completed the following year. Two years later, the Bonart home was listed as a boarding house whose proprietress was widow Bettie Rogers. In 1919 the then remarried Bertha Bonart Lipper sold the house to George Bendizen, who continued renting it out until 1940. New owners restored it back into a single-family dwelling in 1998.

1801 Church
Aaron Levy, who worked for the Blum Hardware Company, built this three-bay-wide Southern townhouse on the corner in 1904.

1804 Church
The first house on the north side of the street, this lavish 1886 Clayton design features a double gallery crowned by a central gable, with a center-hall plan. Still sitting behind its original cast-iron fence, note its extensive gingerbread, befitting Texas' "music man," Thomas Goggan, who owned a state-wide chain of sheet music and instruments stores with his brother.

1816 Church
Houston architect Lewis S. Green built this stuccoed chalet in 1916 for clothing merchant, Henry Tinterow, who marked his house with his initials in its gables over both the house and front steps. Note the four-square home built at the turn of the 20th Century across the avenue at **1815 Church.**

1824 Church
Mrs. John D. Sawyer and her son, William, built this Southern townhouse in 1891. Note the criss-cross pattern in this porch rails and its vaulted gable.

▶ Continue driving west on Church Avenue to begin your first walk in *Beyond the Beaten Paths—the Postoffice Promenade.*

CHAPTER 3

Postoffice Promenade

▶ **Still driving west, cross 19th Street.**

1903 Church

Walking Historic Galveston credits the building of the First Presbyterian Church for bringing famed Victorian master-builder Nicholas J. Clayton to the Island in 1874. He started as

construction supervisor with the Memphis, Tennessee, firm of Jones and Baldwin. After the cornerstone was laid for the church, the chapel fronting the avenue

First Presbyterian Church, 19th and Church

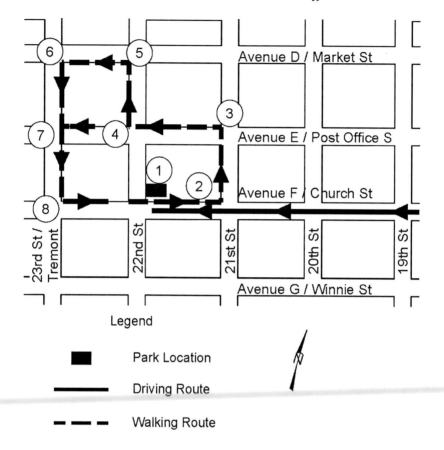

Legend

■ Park Location

——— Driving Route

- - - Walking Route

behind the main sanctuary was completed in 1876 and weekly services began here. However, economic difficulties slowed construction and the church was not consecrated until 1889, with Clayton's own company contributing to its design. For further information about the church and Clayton, please see the walking guide.

2006 and 2010 Church

Across from the rectory of St. Mary's Cathedral, this 1912 boarding house stands next to a more typical mid-century Southern townhouse built in 1867.

▶ **❶** Park your car on the northeast corner of 22nd and Church. You will walk east, against the one-way street.

As the port prospered, Galveston's Central Business District quickly grew, eventually covering approximately 35 square blocks. Covered in chapter one of the walking guide, The Strand and Ship's Mechanic Row primarily housed those businesses connected directly to harbor-related interests, such as commission and wholesale houses, shipping and cotton companies, and banks.

General retailers and professional services located further south on Market and Postoffice. Many of the two and three-storied buildings had their businesses on the ground floor with the owners living quarters above. In many cases, fraternal lodges were located on the upper floors. As time went on, other entities moved in. These included entertainment venues, governmental entities, restaurants, utilities and hotels. Most of the restored buildings in today's Central Business District still have businesses on their first floors with residential lofts or condominiums on their upper stories. Avenue F was appropriately named Church for the number of sacred sanctuaries located along it. The numbered streets on your Postoffice Promenade include 21st and 22nd Streets as well as Tremont.

2128 Church

This corner was the site of Harmony Hall, an elite Jewish social organization, designed by Nicholas Clayton in 1883. Since Galveston was the birthplace of Scotish Rite Freemasonry in Texas, the Masonic San Felipe Lodge of Protection bought the building in 1902 to use as their cathedral. Philip C. Tucker had established the fraternal organization on May 15, 1867, and named it after the first Anglo-American colony in the state. Unfortunately, Clayton's ornate Victorian structure burned down on February 6, 1928. Soon after, President D. W. McLeod named architect H. Jordan MacKenzie of fellow Mason Alfred C. Finn's Houston firm to design a newer and larger cathedral on the same site. Just six months later, the present cathedral was dedicated. Reflecting the popular Art Deco style of the 1920s and '30s, the two-story limestone Cathedral featured a massive arch with carved emblems of the order over its corner entrance, flanked by two copper lanterns and hiding copper doors within. A second entrance on Church is shadowed behind five smaller arches along a stone porch. A two-tiered marble

Harmony Hall, 22nd and Church
—Courtesy of The Rosenberg Library,
Galveston, Texas

staircase, salvaged from Harmony Hall, leads up to the 700-seat auditorium. Hidden within the building is the Egyptian room, a colorfully ornate ceremonial space.

2116 Church

The three-story Electric Service Company showroom, designed by Raymond Rapp in 1927, featured a tapestry brick face and, on the inside, a bronze staircase to its second floor.

2105 Church

W. L. Moody, Jr., bought the corner property at Church and 21st Street from the Elks to build his Jean Lafitte Hotel in 1927. Rising 10 stories, it housed 204 rooms, mostly meant for business travelers. A neoclassical arched brick canopy covered the hotel's entrance. Architect Andrew Fraser, born in Scotland, had immigrated to the United States in 1909, arriving in Galveston just in time to design Mr. Moody's hotel. After standing vacant for two decades, the Jean Lafitte will be converted into apartments, with over 50% reserved for low income tenants.

Across the street to the east, you'll see St. Mary's Cathedral which you'll find in the walking guide. Catty-cornered is the Art Deco **Martini Theatre**, built in 1937. Tied up in probate, its fate is unsure.

St. Mary's Cathedral, 2011 Church

—From the author's collection

▶ ❷ Turn left on 21st Street.

503 21st Street

Architect Donald McKenzie joined with his step brother, C.J.H. Illies, to build a five-story apartment building downtown for rising middle class tenants. They named their investment after their mother, Justine Illies. Opening in 1929, the building housed the Justine Apartments upstairs with retail on the ground floor. The two-story structure to its north was built as a laundry in 1876. Around the corner facing Postoffice, the 1915 League Building was modernized in 1967 with a metal façade and now houses a restaurant.

In the next block to your right, note the 1894 Grand Opera House, marked by its Romanesque arch (in walking guide). Many of these buildings have had their upper floors reborn as residential loft apartments or condominiums during the last twenty years, reverting to their original designs.

The elaborate water fountain on the corner is one of seventeen bequeathed by Henry Rosenberg's estate "for both men and beasts," designed by sculptor J. Massey Rhind. Several have been re-constructed around the city from bits and pieces, using sketches and photographs. This one was funded by Lyda Ann Q. Thomas in honor of her parents, Mr. and Mrs. Arthur W. Quinn.

▶ ❸ **Cross Postoffice (aka Avenue E) and turn left, walking on the north side of the street.**

2102-2106 Postoffice

Investor Marx Marx hired Galveston-born George B. Stowe to design the tan brick Ikelheimer & Co. building. Marx's son-in-law, Nathaniel N. Jacob, owned a crockery store on the first floor so the building was more commonly known as the Jacob Building. Note its corner tower. Next door on the left once stood the imposing two-story Elks Club at **2108**. Damaged during Hurricane Carla in 1961, it was eventually torn down. In 1994, the property was combined with the Jacob Building on the corner and converted into the St. Germain Place condominiums, featuring inside covered parking.

2109 Postoffice

When maintenance costs became prohibitive on their large hall at 22nd and Church, the Harmony Club chose to downsize into a more modest building. In 1895 J. Levy & Brothers funeral directors financed their second Galveston home, designed by N. J. Clayton. The ground floor provided rental income to support the Jewish social club upstairs.

2115 Postoffice

Before it was home to a five-and-dime store, this property housed a candy maker, milliner, and photography shop.

B.P.O.E. (Elks), 2108 Postoffice

—From the author's collection

Patterned after entrepreneur Frank W. Woolworth's original concept, Samuel H. Kress joined the prosperous and growing group in 1896. His Galveston store, built in 1924, reflected the company's standard design for small cities, with its trade mark name centered on the roofline. It remained in business until 1980 when it closed with the other remaining Kresses. It was restored in 1994.

2118-2120 Postoffice

Across the avenue, the Peoples Theater was built for $12,000 in 1908; eight years later, it became the Knights of Columbus property. This Catholic fraternal organization had their meeting rooms on its upper floors, naturally lighted by tall windows, and rental space on its ground floor, like the Harmony Club.

2127 Postoffice

Banker and businessman Henry Beissner built what would house the McCrory's Dime Store on the southeast corner in 1908.

2128 Postoffice

British merchant and ship broker Charles Hodgsen Pix built this pre-Civil War structure, with its distinguished cast-iron windows on its upper floors.

2205 Postoffice Street

The catty-cornered Garbade, Eiband & Co., a landmark in downtown Galveston for years, opened in September 1895. Originally built in 1870 by the Ballinger and Jack law firm, the corner section facing Postoffice housed the Texas Supreme Court from 1875 to 1890. Business was so good for the department store the partners bought the buildings on either side in 1914, and hired Lewis S. Green to consolidate the three, before adding a fourth floor. Mr. Garbade retired in 1920, selling his shares to Mr. Eiband whose sons joined him in the business. Eiband's won acclaim as the most outstanding Department Store in the Southwest, doing business at the same location for 91 years before moving to the Galvez Mall in 1986.

▶ ❹ Cross 22nd Street and turn right.

2200 Postoffice

The Texas Building was constructed as an addition to the Fellman Dry Goods Company to its north. Designed by Charles W. Bulger in 1906, it cost $59,000. The five-story brick structure features a recessed entrance on Postoffice as well as a separate entrance to its upper floors facing 22nd Street on the alley. Clark W. Thompson purchased the business in 1920, naming his new venture after himself. He added the building next door at **2208 Postoffice** to the complex in 1923. A third floor was added to that building seven years later, when it became J. C. Penney's.

2201 Market

The Island City Savings Bank opened here in 1874. Eleven years later, Mr. Harris Kempner invested, followed in 1902 by his sons who bought controlling interests, changing the name to the Texas Bank and Trust Company. They adopted the present name, United States National Bank, in 1923—about the time that eldest son D. W. hired Alfred C. Bossom of England to design a new building. Completed three years later, this eleven-story structure boasted a dark granite base and tall arched windows with a framed corner entrance topped by a clock, befitting a sound financial institution.

▶ ❺ Turn left on Market.

2219 Market City

Chicago architects Weary and Alford squeezed a slender Corinthian exterior to front W. L. Moody's City National Bank in 1920. To compensate, its neo-classical interior featured a barrel-shaped ceiling with gold-leaf plaster work and Italian marble. Ten years after the bank moved around the corner as the Moody National Bank, Mary Moody Northen gave this building to Galveston County to use as a museum. Unfortunately, Hurricane Ike's flood surge closed it.

2221 Market

Designed by architect Thomas H. Adams, who died during its construction, the Tremont Opera House opened at this location on February 25, 1871, closing with the opening of the Grand Opera House on January 3, 1895. Partners Abraham Levy and Leopold Weis owned a clothing and furniture store next door at **2215 Market** in 1877, which became E. S. Levy and Company in 1890. The brothers bought the opera house and hired Alfred Muller to remodel it as a dry goods store. When he died unexpectedly of typhoid, Charles W. Bulger was brought onboard and the remodeling plans changed. The theatre was razed except for its original cast-iron-fronted entry which was incorporated into the new 1896 office building. A fifth floor was added to the E. S. Levy Building four years later. With the store at ground level, the upper stories held various professional businesses, including the U.S. Weather Bureau. During the 1900 Storm, the wind gauge blew away from the roof of this building at 6:30 P.M. after clocking winds at 100 MPH. Later, W. L. Moody, Jr., bought the property and it became known as the National Hotel Building. E. S. Levy continued to lease the first floor until the clothing store moved around the corner to Postoffice in 1917. The building's latest incarnation is as artists' lofts and studios.

▶ ❻ **Turn left on Tremont.**

401-403 Tremont

Across the street, P. N. Comegys designed the corner building in 1869 for T. E. Thompson's "finest jewelry store in the south." Above were "flats" for rent.

▶ ❼ **Turn left on Postoffice.**

2218 Postoffice

Built on the site of the 1868 Chapman & Duffield Bar and Billiard Saloon, the 1880 Clark's building is typical of the smaller brick structures built in Galveston's Central Business District.

Looking east on Postoffice from 23rd Street
—From the author's collection

2214-2216 Postoffice
Houston architect Irving R. Klein designed this building in 1949 for Nathan's Clothing Store which closed in 1975.

▶ **Cross the street to retrace your steps back to Tremont, continuing to walk south.**

2213-2215 Postoffice
This unusual two-story wood-frame building was built in 1885. Mr. Salzmann owned a watch and jewelry store downstairs and lived next to house painter, William J. Houlahan upstairs.

2221-2227 Postoffice
On the corner, Nicholas J. Clayton designed this building for Mrs. Olympia Freybe in 1886 at a cost of $9,000. Thirty-one years later, E. S. Levy and Company moved here from its Market location and continued in business on this corner for 62 years, closing in 1979. On March 13, 1998, a massive fire between its roof and ceiling destroyed most of its Neo-Grec exterior. When repaired, retail shops opened on its ground level, while the upper floors were converted to lofts.

510 23rd Street
Behind the Freybe building on the alley, Clayton also designed this building in 1909 as an annex to that building, matching its façade. His client for this project was Miss Kate Scanlon of Houston. Druggist Charles J. Michaelis moved his 1890 pharmacy, Star Drug Store, here several years later. In 1917 he added a canopy and horseshoe soda fountain/lunch counter. George Clampitt and Grady Dickinson bought the business in 1920 and operated it until 1982. During that time, Star Drug was the first desegregated lunch counter in Galveston. The 1998 fire at the Freybe building spread to the drug store but fortunately, the Galveston Fire Department saved it from major damage. The Tilts family bought the building in November 2001, and began a five-year restoration project. First, they

added two loft apartments on the second floor before they turned their attention to store, soda shop, and lunch counter. Star Drugs re-opened complete with the original neon porcelain Coca Cola sign, horseshoe lunch counter and red tile 5-pointed star logo in summer 2007. Although interrupted by Hurricane Ike, it was back in business by December 2008.

514 Tremont

On the corner stands the Pearce Building with the Wilder Building to its right at **520**. C. D. Hill and Company from Dallas designed the two in 1915, probably at the same time they were working on Galveston's City Hall at Rosenberg and Sealy Avenues. Note the mosaic entry of what is now the Boston Shoe Shop.

▶ **8 Turn left on Church**

2202-2206 Church

The Merrimax Building housed the Southwestern Telegraph and Telephone Company. Built in 1896, it is the only downtown building designed by German-born Alfred Muller. Galveston was the first city in Texas to have telephone service.

Catty-corner across the street, the wall-sized painted advertisement for a nickel Coca Cola was revealed when the corner building, a Sherwin Williams Paint store with the Maye Hotel above, burned down on January 19, 1983—just two weeks after the fire marshal condemned the hotel for fire code violations.

▶ **Crossing 22nd Street, you will find yourself back at your car.**

This concludes your first official walk in *Beyond the Beaten Paths: Driving Historic Galveston.*

CHAPTER 4

Galveston's Victorian East End

North of Broadway

With such a large area to cover, you will complete the East End Historic District north of Broadway first, where the route weaves in and out of its lettered and named streets. However, you will start your drive east via Market from 22nd and Church, where your car was at the end of the previous chapter.

▶ **❶ From the corner of 22nd and Church, drive west to 25th Street (aka Rosenberg Avenue).**

2401 Church
Living upstairs with their mother, brothers David and Michael Jordan ran a corner grocery, crockery and liquor store on this corner, built in 1880. Now a restaurant, note its rear L-shaped wing and sidewalk canopy.

Across the street, Mr. Frederick Schmidt owned a carriage-building company at **2402**.

2406 Church

School teacher James P. Nash built this post-civil war Southern townhouse, Greek Revival in design, as rental property.

▶ **②** **Turn right on 25th Street.**

601 Rosenberg

Designed by Houston architect, Alfred C. Finn, this six-story federal building, housing the Post Office, Custom House and Court House opened in 1937. Texas Cordova fossilated limestone and granite plinth regionalized the façade of its Art Deco design.

513-525 Rosenberg

Across Church Avenue on the northwest corner of 25th Street stands the 1913 Model Laundry and Dye Works building, the city's only modern steam commercial laundry at the time. Prussian immigrant Joseph Finger received his first Galveston

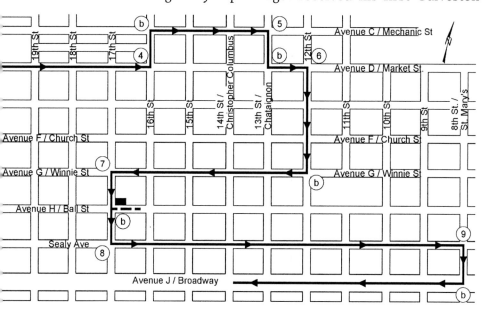

513-25 25th Street (aka Rosenberg Ave)

commissions while partnered with Houston's Lewis Sterling Green. During the 1920s, he would become that city's leading commercial architect. To "fancy-up" this main thoroughfare, he faced the laundry with white glazed brick to contrast with the faded green wooden window and door sashes.

2501–2511 Market

On the west side (on your left) of 25th and Market, note the Hall-Scott buildings designed by George B. Stowe in 1906 and the 1917 Levi building next door.

▶ ❸ Turn right on Market.

Originally Avenue D in the Groesbeck plat, this street was re-named Market for the various "comestible commodities" (i.e., edible products) sold along the avenue, especially between 19th and 21st streets.

2425-2427 Market

The 1878 R. F. Martin and Company Building housed the Variety Saloon on its ground floor in 1885, with a "female boarding house" (i.e., bordello) upstairs.

2419 and 2415 Market

Although neither are his designs, the façades of both the Lalor and Trube buildings demonstrate the influence that Nicholas Clayton exerted on other Galveston architects during the "Gay '90s." Both built in 1894, note the cast-iron storefront of the molded brick, three-story Trube building at **2415**.

2401 Market

Built to replace another consumed by the 1869 fire (see walking guide), this 1870 wood-frame building housed the Central Hotel. Ignoring the city's new fire code mandating that hotels be constructed from noncombustible materials, owner Judge J. L. Darragh claimed this new construction was really a repair.

▶ **Cross 23rd Street, aka Tremont, and continue driving east**

2326-2328, 2322-2324, 2318-2320 and 2314-2316 Market

All four of these uniform buildings were built in 1874: the Dubie, Schulte, A. Flake and Company, and the Engelke buildings respectively.

The next block was covered in Chapter 3, Postoffice Promenade.

1902-1928 Market

Built in 1846 between The Strand and Avenue D, four city lots were shifted to accommodate the city's original Market House at this site. Alfred Muller's first commission on the Island, its ornate, almost over-the-top replacement opened on March 22, 1888. A clock tower centered between two turrets dominated the third floor which housed the Galveston Chamber of Commerce and city offices. The second floor, entered outside via a double-sided winding grand staircase, held City Hall and the police offices, while the market rested at the ground level. Damaged during the 1900 Storm, the building was converted into a fire station. Heavily damaged by Hurricane Carla in 1961, it was demolished four years later—but not before it was featured in a *Route 66* TV show.

In contrast, the massive and stark white American National Insurance Tower at One Moody Plaza replaced the old fire station. Completed in 1971, this 20-story square building, designed by Neuhaus and Taylor of Houston, features a 50 foot high, colonnaded ground floor with underground parking.

Alfred Muller, born in Krefeld, Prussia on September 19, 1855, was a graduate of the Royal Academy of Fine Arts in Berlin, Germany. He came to Galveston in 1886 to work for Nathaniel W. Tobey before establishing his own company the following year. Serving as the chairman of the executive committee of the Texas Association of Architects in 1894-5, he lived with his wife Emilie and their four children at 2111 Avenue M½—just across the avenue from his Galveston Orphan's Home. He died of typhoid fever on June 29, 1896, and was buried in Lakeview Cemetery.

The Gengler Family Grocery Store had stood on the northeast corner of 20th and Market since 1854. Prussian brothers Peter and John had started their business three years earlier from a horse cart. A new, two-story brick building replaced the original wood frame in 1893. After the brothers passed, the sons incorporated the business under Peter's name on May 23, 1898. Maintaining the father's creed of good customer service partnered with the best quality and selection, Gengler's expanded their store to include a bakery in 1908 to become "the largest, finest wholesale and retail grocery in Texas, if not the entire South." Celebrating its 75th Anniversary in 1926, Gengler's ended its run in September 1946, after the last son died without an heir.

402-410 20th Street

Nicholas Clayton designed this subdued building for Bishop Nicholas A. Gallagher in 1888. Named the Catholic Building, it provided meeting rooms upstairs for lay auxiliaries and income-producing rental space on its ground floor.

1921 Market

Born in Germany, John C. Wegner arrived on Galveston Island in 1849, just one year old. He grew up to establish a general store with his brother, Ernest, at the corner of 15th and Avenue K, with the family's living quarters above. They bought this site in 1885 and hired Houston architect Eugene T. Heiner to design the impressive Wegner Brothers market which opened in 1889. Note its six sets of double doors, separated by cast-iron columns. The building became a bakery in 1912, lasting through several owners until 1938.

1801-05 Market

Built in 1898, these twin buildings housed two very different businesses street level with residences above. George Bohn's sheet iron, crockery and hardware business stood on the corner while Charles F. Neuwiller's cabinet shop was to its immediate east.

314 18th Street

Looking to the left down 18th Street, note the gabled, brick Martingano Building, built by Italian shoemaker Michael Martingano in 1914.

402 18th Street

To the right on the corner of 18th Street stands a small church, built in 1926, that originally housed the Swedish Zion Lutheran Church, chartered in 1892. Its original two-story 1895 Chapel served the congregation until William Kahlew designed the present sanctuary, complete with a pipe organ and stained glass.

1704 Market

Standing one block east, this house was moved to this location by Irish baker Christopher Fox right after the Great Fire of 1885. While the city slept in the early morning hours of Friday, November 13, a strong north wind fueled a smoldering fire accidently left burning at the Vulcan Ironworks at 16th and The Strand. Jumping from rooftop to rooftop, the flames destroyed a total of 40 square blocks of homes by morning. A tremendous building boom ensued in the residential "Fire District" over the next ten years. As for the Fox house, Nicholas Clayton expanded it in 1888 with wrap-around galleries and a bay above the entrance on 17th Street. Cast iron railings replaced wooden ones during the 1920s.

1613 Market

Built for the family of furniture store owner, Mr. John H. Meyers in 1904, this late Victorian features a turret and a gable. Across the street, note the large modified Greek Revival at **1614** built in 1886.

1622 Market

Sharing a full lot split in two, this slender, high-raised Southern townhouse replaced one that burned during the 1885 fire, as did its neighbor at **1614**. Cotton screwman and builder Gustave Johnson lived here only two years before he passed. Used as rental property by its second owner, William Ansley, the house changed hands again in 1906 when Madeline V. Lipanovich bought it.

In 1909 she opened John's Oyster Resort, on breezy Offats Bayou with her brother-in-law John Lozica and his brother Nick. After the original building was destroyed in a fire, the restaurant was rebuilt in 1928 as "Casablanca-style." At age 49, "Aunt Mollie" died unexpectedly the following year and both house and business passed to the Lozica family. Serving until 1986, the building on the bayou briefly became a Mexican restaurant before it was reincarnated as a church, only to be demolished during the spring of 2009.

▶ ❹ **Turn left on 16th Street and left on Mechanic.**

Also called Ship's Mechanic Row, this original Avenue C got this name "because of the number of craftsman shops located on it," according to *Galveston Daily News* reporter Lillian Herz on October 14, 1962. The structures in this particular neighborhood typify the city during the mid-19th century, before the Victorian era.

1527 Mechanic

On the corner of 16th and Mechanic stands an 1871 Greek Revival Southern townhouse. Its wide double gallery is supported by four columns, with walk-through windows and a centered entry topped by a transom and sidelights. Ship captain William B. Hance lived here with his wife Emma and son Willie.

1524 Mechanic

Built for City Marshall John H. Westerlage in 1859, this two-story house was most typical of early Galveston neighborhoods.

1508 Mechanic

Publisher Robert C. Johnson bought this circa 1870 Gulf Coast cottage twenty years later, listing it as both his residence and business. Among his publications was *The Opera Glass* which was a "society and family paper," according to the *Galveston Architecture Guide*.

1428 Mechanic

This compact one-story cottage appears to have been moved to the side yard of the house next door, but when and the year it was built is unknown.

1427 Mechanic

A three-bay Southern townhouse stands on the corner.

1424 Mechanic

One of the larger homes on the block, this Civil War era residence was owned by Hezekiah Wilson.

1412 Mechanic

Ice importer George H. Delesdernier lived in this 1865 two-story with his family.

301 14th Street

Built with donated funds in 1989, the magnificent Ronald McDonald House, a homey hostel, provides housing for low-income families who could not otherwise afford to stay in Galveston while their children are in treatment at U.T.M.B. Houston architects Gayle and Joe Adams incorporated Victorian elements in its postmodern design to conform to the integrity of the city's East End.

214 14th Street

On this property once stood the "Starter Home" of stevedore James S. Waters, who became "Lord" of the 1100 block of Church at the turn of the 20th Century. Unfortunately, his dilapidated three-bay-wide cottage was demolished in 2012.

▶ ❺ **Turn right on 13th Street back to Market, and turn left.**

You'll find information about the Rosenberg home to your right and, across the avenue, the Runge house in *Walking Historic Galveston*.

1221 Market

According to tax records, locksmith Robert Ohring built this side-gabled clapboard cottage with a small front porch as rental property around 1872. However, the placement of its "clipped" eaves—i.e., pressed tightly against the wall rather than extending beyond it—indicate an earlier, perhaps 1850's house on Galveston Island.

1217 Market

Sitting on two lots, this five-bay-wide raised cottage featured a single-bay entry porch centered beneath twin dormers with its front door framed by a transom and sidelights. A bookkeeper for several downtown firms, Frederick Martini built the home circa 1871 for his wife Minna and son Fred Jr. An office boy for the Texas Star Flour Mill, their son moved out in 1897, when he got a better job with the Mexican Telephone Company. After her husband died suddenly on November 26, 1891, Minna lived here until 1913, when the house was sold to James Boyle, a ship captain and pilot. He renovated the windows and added the small room on its east side. Herman and Elise Futterhecker bought the property in 1922 and raised three children here. In 1941 his widow sold it to prominent neurosurgeon Dr. Samuel R. Snodgrass, who lived here for the next fourteen years, after which the house suffered as rental property until 2002, when it was restored.

▶ **❻ Across from the modern University of Texas Medical Branch campus, turn right on 12th Street. Crossing both Postoffice and Church, which were featured in Chapter 2, turn right again on Winnie and continue driving west to 17th Street.**

Listed on the Groesbeck city plat as Avenue G, this street was named after Gilbert Winnie, the first white liveryman on the Island. He and his wife Charlotte resided on the northwest corner of 20th and Winnie until his death in 1860. His house was torn down during the 1890s to make way for a Catholic school.

1209 Winnie

Medard Menard came to Galveston in 1837 to help his uncle, Michel B. Menard, establish the city. Returning from the Civil War as a Confederate colonel, he was appointed "Cotton Weigher." In 1882 he built this dormered, five-bay-wide cottage for himself and his widowed daughter Mrs. J. B. (Marie) Lancton, who was born in 1839 to become the first "white girl" BOI. She lived here until her death in 1899, and the house sold to jeweler Herbert and Bertha Ganter in 1902. Note its Eastlake-detailed porch. Across the avenue, note the 1922 Craftsman bungalow at **1208**.

The 1300 Block of Winnie

The two-storied, high raised Victorian houses on the south side of this street illustrate the economy of space and uniformity used for rental property during the 1890s. William Stephenson built **1317** and **1319** in 1893, then **1321** four years later. In 1891, Henry D. Schulte built **1316** on the north side of the street, and the other two nine years later.

1414 Winnie

This Arts and Crafts home, built in 1907, featured a wraparound front porch. With its horizontal orientation, it offers a nod toward the "modern" Prairie style, popularized by Frank Lloyd Wright.

1420 Winnie

Note the double gallery of this 1869 Victorian.

1512 and 1510 Winnie

Developer Christian J. Henck built these tenant houses in 1879.

1515 Winnie

Tax records indicate that the Charles F. Kuers family owned the property as early as 1890. Even though the City of Galveston sold it at public auction for back taxes in 1903, his daughter

Amelia inherited it five years later. She married foundryman William J. Cain and they hired contractor M. C. Bowden to build a home of their own. An eclectic mixture of Federalist and Colonial Revival with Victorian gingerbread, the modest two-story frame house remained in the Cain family until the widow Amelia passed in 1956. When this "blue collar" home was restored, elements of Eastlake were added to the mix.

1520-1518 Winnie

Mirror images of each other, the side halls of these rentals are located on the climatically warmer side as breezes typically blew in from the east. They were built in 1915 by Dr. Cooper P. Bevil.

1522 Winnie

Police officer George W. Morris built this large Gulf Coast cottage around 1876.

1605 Winnie

Across the street stands an 1892 Victorian. Note its single centered dormer and gable.

1608 Winnie

While information about the Senecals' home/corner store at **1602** can be found in the walking guide, this house was constructed as a tenant house in 1907; its twin at **1606** followed four years later. Louis W. and his wife Rosa bought the lot from developer Maud Moller three years earlier. Born in New Orleans, Senecal learned the grocery business working for Peter Gengler, before he opened up his own neighborhood shop in 1901.

1616 Winnie

This Italianate house, with its small Ionic pillars, was built for school teacher Miss Mathilda Wehmeyer during the reconstruction of the 1885 fire district.

1617 Winnie

Across the street, note the fancy mansard roof of the 1886 Charles I. Kory home.

▶ **❼ Turn left on 17th Street, then another left on Ball Avenue.**

While information about the west side of the block is included in the walking guide, the 1600 block of Ball is rich with hidden historical treasures. You might want to **park and walk it**. Originally named Avenue H, this street was renamed after businessman-turned-philanthropist George Ball.

1622 Ball

Typical of the Galveston style, this double-galleried house combines the simplicity of Greek Revival with the fancy "gingerbread" (i.e., wooden millwork or intricate decorative trim) of a truly Victorian home. Built by George W. Trapp, it replaced another that was destroyed in the Great Fire of 1885. Trapp worked as a bookkeeper for Moritz Kopperl's coffee import firm. During that time, Galveston became the fourth leading coffee port in the United States.

1616 and 1614 Ball

Tailor John F. Michels built both of these gabled houses in 1886, one to replace another reduced to ashes during the great fire that previous November and the other as rental property.

1617 Ball

German tailor Adolph and Lena Nitschke lived at this address in a small house next to St. Paul's German Presbyterian Church. They built this large two-story home in 1886 to replace one lost in the fire. Although he died on June 5, 1900, at age 64, his widow remained here, even though this house was "wrecked" during the 1900 Storm and quickly repaired. Lena sold it to T. C. Davis in 1914, who later sold it to John and Ann Winchester in 1937. Born in Chicago on December 28, 1907, this businessman invested in Galveston's beachfront and served as the city's finance commissioner from 1955-57. Ann, a "BOI," volunteered at UTMB Children's Hospital until her death in 1988.

1612 Ball

The First Presbyterian Church built this three-bay Southern townhouse in 1890 as its parsonage. Note its differing lintels between the veranda posts on both floors.

1612 Ball

You will find both **1601 and 1602 Ball** in *Walking Historic Galveston* which covers that avenue to 13th Street.

▶ Retrace your steps back to your car.

▶ ❽ Back in your car, turn left on 17th Street, then another left on Sealy, driving eastward to 8th Street.

Named after the prominent city family, this most prestigious street was originally known as Avenue I. Again, the buildings on the west side of the street are listed in the walking guide.

1627 Sealy

John Clement Trube of Denmark sailed into Galveston Bay in 1848 to work at a Houston grocery business. He married Verona Durst from a prominent Texas family on December 31,

1860, and moved to Galveston eight years later, where most of their six children were born. By the time he was 35 years old, he had enough real estate holdings both on the Island and in Houston to retire. To build the family home in 1890, he hired Alfred Muller who based his design on Trube's memories of a castle in Keil. "The strangest house in a city of strange houses," the Trube Castle was restored in 1989, based on its original blueprints which were found in the newel post at the bottom of the stairs.

1620 Sealy

Designed by J. H. Jordan, this high-raised gabled Colonial Revival with its Doric columns was built in 1896 by commission broker Louis Marx and his wife, Rachael. They lived here until 1905, when he took a job as a traveling salesman and the family moved to Houston. When Louis moved out, older brother Marx's family moved in, living here for eight more years. The Marx family was a prominent Galveston merchant family. The elder Marx had partnered with Mr. Kempner in 1871 to establish a successful wholesale grocery and liquor store; he would also partner with his son-in-law Abe Blum 21 years later in a wholesale boots, shoes, and hats business. The house changed hands several more times until pilot boat Captain Lewis Locke moved in to stay until his death in 1944. Although the post-Ike detailed wood carving, entitled "The Birds of Galveston" appears to be on the city sidewalk of the next house, brochures list this as its address.

1610 Sealy

Cotton merchant and president of the Gulf City Compress, Henry W. Hackbarth started building this Craftsman home for his growing family in 1915 but construction was interrupted by the 1915 storm. After a hurricane in 1918 destroyed 36,000 bales of cotton in his warehouse, Hackbarth was forced to declare bankruptcy and moved to Waco. The house changed hands many times over the years. Its most illustrious tenant was Del Pratt, part of the New York Yankees' "Murderers' Row" with Babe Ruth in 1920, who lived there from 1936 to 1941.

Next door on the corner stood the Heidenheimer Castle, de-

1610 Sealy

signed by Nicholas Clayton in 1857, but extensively remodeled and enlarged in 1887 and 1890 respectively. Even more unusual than the Trube house, this grand home burned in 1973 and was demolished three years later.

1609 Sealy
One of two tenant houses, Henry M. Trueheart built this twin-dormered, raised cottage in 1886, which backed up to his Broadway turreted mansion.

902 16th Street
The original owner of this property was John Corbett whose daughter, Eliza, inherited it in 1884. Upon her death in 1895, her sister, Mrs. Francis Robbins sold the mostly unimproved

land to the Liebermans who sold it to Morris Stern in 1907. This successful wholesale grocer built the Neo-Classical mansion the following year. A perfect example of the grandeur of Colonial Revival, this respectable home features two Corinthian columns supporting a gabled portico. Although it appears to be constructed of cut stone, its exterior façade is actually a "rusticated" finish: crushed oyster shells and concrete mixed with water, and then sculpted over either brick or wood frame.

1514 Sealy

Duhamel and Lawler designed this Victorian chalet for Judge George E. Mann in 1877. Note its arched entry, double front doors and single-story veranda.

1509 Sealy

With rear wings on both sides, this raised cottage features a one-bay-wide centered front porch approachable by a double stair case. Henry W. Bentinck built it circa 1866.

1503 Sealy

Reminiscent of New Orleans' Garden District, this classic Victorian Southern townhouse was built for coppersmith and gas fitter, Joseph Brockelman in 1873. Note the cobalt and cranberry stained glass in the first floor windows. Druggist T. C. Thompson added them while he owned the house.

1426-1428 Sealy

Born in Hanover, Germany, Julius H. Ruhl hired Chicago architect T. J. Overmire to design this five-bay-wide, double-galleried Victorian Neo-Grec classic in 1875. A respected partner in the prestigious firm of Kaufmann and Runge, he died a mysterious death in October of that year after it was discovered that he had "speculated" with $20,000 of company money. After drinking himself ill at a bar, his strychnine-laded body was found at an old, deserted bath house three hours later. Some believe that the double-decker widow's walk was original to Overmire's only design on the Island. The large house certainly stands in stark contrast to the bricked Robert M. Gunther bungalow next door (**1418**), designed by Raymond Rapp in 1929.

1428 Sealy

1417 Sealy

Irish architect John DeYoung came to Texas via New York in 1837 to work on the republic's provisional capital. By 1846, he was serving as Galveston's City Surveyor when he built this flat-roofed classical Greek Revival house—another of the oldest in the East End—which he sold to J. Carroll Smith in 1859. The house, however, was named for its third owner: a most colorful character, professional soldier Thomas Chubb, who came to Texas to fight in its War of Independence from Mexico. He became a harbor pilot, protecting Galveston Bay. During the Civil War, he was captured by the Union and imprisoned in a New York jail. Family legend has it that his daughter Cecelia watched the Battle of Galveston on January 1, 1863, from its flat roof. After the Secretary of the U.S. Navy released him, Chubb returned home and sold his house in 1867.

1416 Sealy

Two years before her corner house was built, Mrs. E. Ruhl had this three-dormered, Gulf Coast tenant cottage constructed for neighbor Captain Steinbark. Although much of Ruhl's estate was liquidated as reparation, his widow retained ownership of both homes on Sealy, finally selling this cottage to A. J. Henck in 1913.

1411 and 1417 Sealy with Bishop's Palace in background

1411 Sealy

Across the street stands the Diocese of Galveston Chancery Building, built in 1924. After Bishop Byrne bought the Gresham House on Broadway from Walter's widow for $40,500 (see the walking guide), he had this small, stuccoed Mission-style office building constructed. Note its red clay-tiled roof and brick-lined scalloped gable.

1412 Sealy

Young Galveston businessman, August J. Henck, built this charming raised Victorian cottage, with Queen Anne elements, in 1897. Note its chamfered gable, turned columns and stained glass windows. The son of German immigrants, August never married but adopted a daughter named Sadie, who ran her father's business. She died in 1960, leaving a trust to expand the "Roman Catholic religious, educational and charitable purposes in Texas."

▶ Carefully cross the well-traveled 14th Street

1318 Sealy

C. W. Bulger designed this picturesque, multi-gabled Victorian in 1896 for banker William C. Skinner. Legend has it that noises in the attic prompted resident Althea Wade to set rat traps. What she caught was a gold-headed walking cane inscribed, "J. D. Skinner, November 6, 1895"—the builder's father.

1316 and 1314 Sealy

When her father, marble contractor Alexander Allen (who lived further east on the avenue) gave her these two lots, daughter Marcia Aiken built this pair of Southern townhouses circa 1876 as rental properties. Both feature gabled-fronts supported by octagonal columns.

1310 Sealy

Owner of the Galveston Garage, one of three automobile repair businesses on the Island in 1909, Fernand Lobit bought this high raised home that sits on 11-foot piers. A three-car garage housed his cars behind the residence. In 1910, Lobit leased the house for three years to Harry Black, who took over the Blum Hardware Company, renaming the business after himself. Lobit sold the house in 1917.

1228 Sealy

During the early 1870s, Lemuel Burr, a traveling salesman with the wholesale dry goods company Leon and H. Blum, bought this lot and ½ from John Beissner. Designed by Nicholas J. Clayton, this 1876 Victorian townhouse featured Italianate and Gothic details in its ornate gingerbread. Seven years later, he sold the home to Julius Kauffman, a partner in the largest cotton exporting firm in Galveston. His wife, Clara, sold it to Captain James Perrie Alvey in 1890. A Confederate veteran under General Stonewall Jackson and in the Battle of Gettysburg, he served as vice president of the Galveston Wharves, director of the First National Bank and chairman of the first Grade Raising Board. Split into apartments over the years, the house was restored as a single-family dwelling in 1980. The current owners added a wood sculpture of their Great Dane, Lewis, which usually changes costumes with the seasons!

On the south side of the street, note **1223 Sealy** which was built in 1915, and the 1875 raised cottage at **1213** with its side-facing dormers.

1212 Sealy

Local cotton broker George Bondies built this charming twin-gabled Victorian/Eastlake in 1877. Nine years later, he sold it to Joseph Archibald Robertson, who remodeled it for his family of nine children. Standing behind a concrete iron fence, note the detail on its double galleries, accented by its paint job. In 1904, this president of the People's Loan and Homestead and commissioner of the port's pilots, added a two-story garage "for an electric automobile" with servants' rooms above.

1204 Sealy

A partner in the law firm of Wheeler and Rhodes, Henry W. Rhodes built this "folk" Victorian home in 1877. The house changed hands many times over the years. Owner of Bart Lumber Company, Fred and his wife Mary Barthelme bought it in 1922 and made many major improvements in the 28 years they lived here. They sold this home in 1950 and moved to San Antonio, but soon returned to the Island to live in Cedar Lawn. Although he did design one house on the Island (see the next chapter on your way to the Broadway Cemetery), son Donald became well respected for his modern architectural designs in Houston. And his son Donald Jr. grew to be an accomplished novelist at the University of Houston.

1205 Sealy

Owned by Mrs. M. W. Thomas during the 1900 Storm, this gabled cottage lists to the west—perhaps a leftover of the hurricane's damage.

▶ **Continue driving east to 8th Street**

1123 Sealy

Henry Graugnard paid just $275 for this simple 1902 Colonial Revival cottage which was moved from 1203 Avenue L, near the family bakery. Although rented to wholesale coffee dealer

Charles C. Bailey, Henry's eldest son, Edward, chose it as his honeymoon home when he married Elizabeth Shram of Dallas. In 1923, his father deeded it to them after their first child—a boy—was born. When he grew up, he would continue the family's bakery business. Edward's widow, Elizabeth, lived here until she died at age 92 in 1983—73 years in one house!

1122 Sealy

This Greek Revival with its three-bay front porch and gabled windows was built in 1866. Carpenter William Best started the house in February and his wife, Catherine, sold that "improved property" to her brother and sister-in-law five months later. Louis and Anne Best continued their own improvements until 1871, when they sold it to brick mason Thomas Lucas and his wife, Catherine. The property changed hands many times over the years, ending as rental property. During the 1980s, it was scheduled to the razed when it was reborn through restoration.

1122 Sealy

1118 Sealy

Although this site is listed on the tax rolls as early as 1840, a house did not stand here until 1876, when Alexander Allen built his residence. The simple two-story Greek Revival featured double inset galleries both back and front. He and his business partner, Charles Ott, owned a successful marble company bearing the Allen name. To commemorate the Battle of San Jacinto in South Houston, Allen Monuments erected a 15½-foot blue marble monument in 1881. After his death the following year, Allen's widow married her husband's partner, who promptly changed the company's name to the Ott Monument Works, now Texas' oldest monument company.

1110 Sealy

Allen left this lot to his widowed daughter, Sarah E. Bennett, to be developed as rental property. Her sister Marcia E. Aiken supervised the construction of this charming Stick style house in 1887. In charge of the family's investments, she sold it to watchmaker Mac Alfish in 1910, who replaced the original porch with a Colonial Revival veranda. The house next door at **1114** was once part of the Allen house. W. L. Garbode, a partner with the Eibands' in a dry goods store on Postoffice (see Chapter 3), remodeled it in 1915.

1109 Sealy

Henry C. Eiband hired R. R. Rapp to build this brick, cubic Colonial Revival in 1927.

1102 Sealy

Originally built in 1879 by coal distributor Frank A. Park, this expansive house was enlarged in 1896 by J. Henry Langbehn, a shipping agent. Note that it is raised on an arched basement.

901 11th Street

Located on the southwest corner, Nathan V. Morgan of the American National Insurance Company built this house circa 1922.

1003 Sealy

Brothers Adolph and Sebastian Drouet came to Galveston from France in 1842. Both earned their living ferrying cargo and passengers across Galveston Bay and both fought in the Texas Navy during the Civil War. Although they bought this property in 1866, it wasn't until 1892 that Sebastian built a four-room cottage here, which was destroyed during the 1900 Storm. His son Charles built the present five-room Queen Anne in 1903.

913 and 915 Sealy

African American Horace Scull, a carpenter who fought for black education after the Civil War, constructed these two raised shotgun houses to replace two swept away during the 1900 Storm. The name of this Southern style, primarily inhabited by low-income families, comes from legend, which said that one could fire a shotgun through the front door and the bullet would exit out the back door without hitting any interior walls.

807 and 809 Sealy

Another name for this style of cottage is "commissary house," which were meant as temporary housing after the hurricane. These two are typical of this type, with their small front porches, hipped roofs and simple Victorian gingerbread. George Edwards built them between 1906 and 1908 to replace two others destroyed during the 1900 Storm. The houses next door at **813**, **815**, and **817** were constructed by his brother Charles, who was a house painter.

▶ ❾ Turn right on 8th Street, then right again on Broadway

808 Broadway

John Arthur "aka Jack" Johnson, the World's Heavy Weight champion from 1908 to 1915, was born at this address on March 28, 1878. The house, however, was washed away during the 1900 Storm and replaced with this shot-gun cottage.

926 Broadway

The large, two-story home near the corner of 10th and Broadway was given to the W. Ellis Badgett family after the

Mrs. gave birth to quadruplet girls on February 1, 1939. "B.O.I." at St. Mary's Infirmary, Joyce, Jeraldine (Jerry), Jeanette (Jenny) and Joan charmed their way into the national spotlight, bringing their coastal hometown with them. Cameras and Fox Movietone News followed "Galveston's Sweethearts" as they served as honorary flower girls for Alice Fay when she married Phil Harris at the Hotel Galvez in 1941, through birthdays and Christmases—even as they helped sell War Bonds during World War II. "The 4 J's" posed with Tarzan Johnny Weissmuller during the city's 1946's "Splash Day," and were named honorary Girl Scouts and Texas "Rangerettes." Off the Island, the quads flew to New York to appear on the game show, "What's My Line?" Older sister Elsie Mae, then 14 years old, remembered that living with the sweethearts was like "playing with living dolls."

926 Broadway, Badgett quads
—Courtesy of Elsie Badgett Graugnard and family

1114 Broadway

German immigrant Joseph Boddeker fought for the Texas Navy in the Battle of Galveston on January 1, 1863, earning the title, Captain. His wife, Carrie Behlin, bore him eight sons. When his original home on this site was destroyed during the 1900 Storm, Captain Boddeker bought a structurally-sound 1880 house at 12th and Sealy and had it moved here using logs and horses, then made extensive repairs. After he died in 1905, his widow continued to live in the house with her son Tony's family. Active in local politics, he created the state Commission for the Blind and served as one of its first members. The family continued to live in the home for over ninety years.

1201-3 Broadway

On the south side of the street, the green-tiled roof and gabled front porch further enhances this large stucco-faced Spanish Mission design. Typical of the Island's Roarin' Twenties elite, Kempner cotton exporter Herman and Mildred Nussbaum built it in 1920—according to a descendant.

1202 Broadway

Manager of the Gulf Fisheries Company, Willoughby J. Chapman built this simple wood-frame house in 1903. Two years later, he updated the simple Victorian by adding a Queen Anne style porch.

1210 Broadway

Notice the delightful double galleries of druggist F. George Leinback's 1906 home. Note that the decorative cement parapet still surrounds the vacant lot next door, once site of Mrs. Elise Michael's N. J. Clayton 1884 design.

1309 Broadway

Captain Thomas S. Dignan built this Gulf Coast cottage on the south side of the street circa 1867. His neighbor Captain James McDonald worked for him as a skipper during the 1850s, sailing the Gulf as far as Tampico, Mexico.

1313 Broadway

This five-bay-wide Greek Revival cottage was originally built by a Scottish born sailor in 1869 for his wife, Annie Schwann. In 1873, "Capt. Jim" became a Galveston harbor pilot. He sold it to another sea captain, John McCall, ten years after the house was built. During the 1890s, McCall updated it by adding fish scale shingles and Victorian gingerbread on the porch, which was severely damaged during the 1900 Storm.

1317 Broadway

"B.O.I" contractor Edwin Paul Anonsen began construction of his house in 1944 while he and his wife Delpha lived in the pre-existing garage apartment. In contrast to its Victorian neighbors, its offset entrance beneath a flat roof features round windows suggestive of a ship's wheel and portholes. Anonsen sold the home in 1961 when he built another at 1205 Harbor View Drive.

▶ **Half-way through your drive through Galveston's historic East End, you will turn left to explore south of Broadway.**

. . . and South

▶ **1** **From Broadway, turn left on 14th Street, crossing into the Lost Bayou District.**

This official historic district runs approximately from 21st to 14th Streets, Avenues K–M½. From its eastern boundary, you will wander in and out of the larger San Jacinto area during this East End drive. Readers will find more information about that district as well as the Bishop's Palace, Sacred Heart and 1403 Broadway structures in *Walking Historic Galveston: A Guide to its Neighborhoods*.

1111 14th Street
On the right stands a small two-bay wide cottage which was built circa 1875.

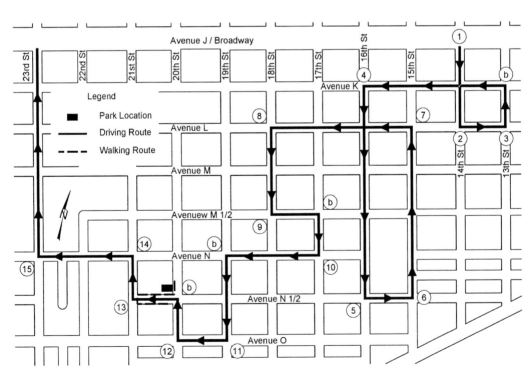

▶ ❷ **Turn left on Avenue L**

1328 Avenue L

Nevertheless sorely in need of restoration, this unique 1895 raised cottage features a side-gable roof and twin attic dormers with unusual finials pointing up to heaven. What a picturesque potential as a weekend home or rental!

1301 Ave L

The St. Luke's Missionary Baptist Church was built in 1911 and remains a neighborhood landmark.

1227 Avenue L

On the corner to your right stands the Art Deco G & G Bakery. Born in Barcelonette, France, teenager Henry Graugnard earned his passage across the Atlantic by learning how to bake. Landing in Mexico, he moved to Galveston in 1884 to open his own bakery. With his new wife, French-Canadian Pauline Louiselle, they opened a French bakery at this location in 1888, while living next door. After the 1900 Storm destroyed it, the elder Graugnard rebuilt the bakery and enlisted his two sons, Edward and Henry, to help with deliveries by horse-drawn cart. This was replaced by a fleet of brightly-painted trucks during the 1930s. After their father died in 1937, the brothers partnered, renaming the business G & G Bakery and, three years later, built this streamlined baking plant, marked by glass blocks crowning the entry.

▶ ❸ **Turn left on 13th Street, then left again on Avenue K**

1314 Avenue K

Built in 1875, this two-story Southern townhouse with its three bays supported by columns overshadows the small shot gun cottages and bungalows surrounding it.

1328 Avenue K

On the corner of 14th and Avenue K stands the 1892 Ernest Wegner house. As a child, Wegner emigrated from Germany around 1850. He and his brother, John, established a success-ful grocery store down 14th Street on Postoffice. Quitting the business in 1882, he went into politics, first serving as county commissioner, then fire chief. Designed by Houston architect Eugene T. Heiner, Wegner built this Queen Anne for his wife Christiana and their five children. Suffering no damage during the Great Storm of 1900, it served as a refuge for 150 people. However, its original design was greatly modernized with tai-lored Arts and Crafts features during 1933.

▶ **Cross 14th Street and drive west to 16th Street**

1406 Avenue K
This small 1891 cottage is most typical of those in this area of the city.

1417 Avenue K
Originally built in 1882, this three-dormered Victorian features a pointed tower and bay window on its east side. Both were added by bank bookkeeper, Herman Riedel, during the late 1890s.

1424, 1426, and 1428 Avenue K
Architect Alfred Muller built triplet two-story Southern town-houses in 1895 on two city lots divided into thirds on "spec." Offering them while they were being built allowed potential homeowners to customize their interiors. Each distinctive in its own subtle way, note that **1426** stands taller than the other two as its owner was the only one who elected to lift his home during the grade raising.

1501 Avenue K
Along with its neighbor at **1505**, this five-bay-wide cottage was built in 1867 sans front porch, which was common for that time. It was probably added after the 1900 Storm.

1519 Avenue K
This large-scale, stand-out Greek Revival, circa 1870, featured Doric columns. Heavily damaged during the 1900 Storm, it was extensively repaired in 1901 by John Goggan. Along with

his brother Thomas, who lived north of Broadway at 1804 Church (see Chapter 2), they specialized in everything musical.

1524 Avenue K

Carpenter Christopher Schmidt built this Greek Revival cottage in 1867-68 at the corner of 16th and K. Moved one block east to this site after the 1900 Storm, note its impressive dormers above its centered, gabled front porch.

▶ **④ Turn left on 16th Street, driving south 5 blocks to Avenue N½.**

You'll find the Lasker Home across 16th Street on your right, the city's newest Bed and Breakfast, in the walking guide.

1113-15 16th Street

The two-story on the alley was built in 1897.

1601 Avenue M

This five-bay-wide home, built by Charles Engelke in 1883, featured a two-storied front porch centered beneath twin dormers. Owner of a hardware store, tinning and cornice manufacturing business, he incorporated punched tin cornices on his house, which have disappeared over time. When built, the Engelke home sat next to one of the grandest residences in town: crockery merchant A. C. Crawford's country house, built in 1867, which was gone by 1882.

1523, 1525 and 1527 Avenue M

On your left, Dr. David H. Lawrence built these three tenant houses in 1910. Note the gabled roofs over their single-story porches.

▶ **⑤ Turn left on Avenue N½.**

Crossing Avenue M½, you have entered the San Jacinto area, which spreads south of Broadway from 23rd (or Tremont) Street east to 6th.

1514 Avenue N½

Four blocks further south rising high above this working-class neighborhood stands **Stephen F. Austin Junior High School**. Designed by Houston architect Ben Milam in 1939, its horizontal three-tiered symmetry stands tallest over its entry, complete with Art Deco relief. Perhaps courtesy of the Public Works Administration, the panel depicts the industrial sides to living on an Island: oil derricks, cotton bales, the Port—all basking beneath a glowing sun.

1514 Ave N½ (Stephen F. Austin Jr. High)

▶ ❻ Turn left on 15th Street.

Note that many houses in this working-class neighborhood are undergoing somewhat of a rebirth through restoration. Perhaps the stories of these homes will soon be revealed . . . ? Back in the Lost Bayou District, look to your right toward the middle of the block at the intersection of 15th and L.

1414 Avenue L

Most of this "old" Gulf Coast dormered cottage dates from 1865-70, even though there is speculation that the front porch probably was not added until 1892.

1201 15th Street

African American, George Edwards, owned this early (circa

1860s) worker's cottage and rented it to working class families and single women of his race. With its gabled front, notice its stylized shutters and dormers on its Avenue L side, suggesting a recently-added second floor above its "pushed out" north wall. The screened porch connects with a second cottage on its south side to further increase the living space.

▶ **❼ Turn left on Avenue L.**

1502 Avenue L

Arriving in Galveston in the mid-1870s, the Potthoff family have resided on this northwest corner of Avenue L since 1875, according to city directories. However, there is much confusion through the years about first names and relationships, so it seems that even documented records cannot be trusted to tell the truth! An "old" one-story residence with a basement, wooden cistern and single-story "barn" (a hen house, perhaps?) in the back yard stood here in 1902; however, three years later, it had been replaced by the current two-story Southern town-house. Its side-hall design incorporated the passage along the

1502 Ave L

length of its west side to shield the east side living quarters against the hot afternoon sun—a necessity in pre-air conditioning days! The current owners have added a rear wing with yard space to create a serene, classic corner refuge to anchor this historic neighborhood.

▶ **Continue driving west on Avenue L**

1602, 1604, and 1606 Avenue L

The three two-story houses on the north side of the street started as one-story raised cottages in 1897. Their owner chose to raise their outdoor basements and enclose them, thus adding a new ground floor, to accommodate more tenants.

1607 Avenue L

Across the avenue, this 1890 home started as a 1½ story Colonial. After it floated off its foundations during the Great Storm of 1900, its owner raised the ground floor up, inserting a new one beneath in 1906.

To your right on the northeast corner of the avenue and 17th stands a tenant house built in 1883—a survivor of the Great Fire of 1885.

1207, 1209, and 1211 17th Street

Look to your left down the street to find three shotgun cottages. They may have been pre-fab commissary houses, which were used as emergency housing after the 1900 hurricane.

1710 Avenue L

This raised tenant cottage, crowned by a small gable, was built in 1888 by Mrs. Charlotte Krohn. In the next block on the south side of the street stand two very similar cottages at **1809** and **1813**, built perhaps by Mrs. Krohn's widowed sister.

▶ **❽ Turn left on 18th Street.**

To include all of the few-&-far between sites in this Lost Bayou District within the large San Jacinto area, the route is quite circuitous.

1211 18th Street

Butcher Conrad Lena originally built his 1891 home on the corner; however, this unusual design was moved to the back yard while maintaining its mansard roof and three-story squared tower.

You will find all four corner houses at the intersection of 18th and Avenue M—numbers 1726-28, 1725, 1801 and 1806 — in *Walking Historic Galveston*.

▶ ❾ Turn left on Avenue M½, then right on 17th Street

You will cross into the San Jacinto area for the remainder of your drive.

1710 Avenue M½

Between 1875 and 1880, farmer Julius Loebenstien built six raised rectangular houses and one small L-shape cottage on the northeast corner of 18th Street, moving to this block from the country to the city in 1881.

17th and Avenue M ½

1628 Avenue M½
Originally built as the German Methodist Episcopal Church in 1909, this Victorian folk structure featured a tower topped by a candle-snuffer steeple.

▶ ⑩ Turn right on Avenue N.

This street was also named Ursuline after the convent of nuns that stood further west, set back from, but facing the avenue between 25th and 27th streets.

▶ ⑪ Two blocks west, turn left on 19th Street and drive south another two blocks to the one-way Avenue O. The next two addresses are ½ block before you make that turn.

1612 19th Street
On your left stands an 1890s high-raised bungalow.

1611 19th Street
Across the street, city tax collector Ira E. Collin built this unique raised cottage in 1899, the same year listed for its neighbor. Note how these two tenant houses seem to guard the alley entrance.

1613 19th Street
This house, built by bookkeeper Daniel W. Nettleton, extends over the alley to increase the square footage. Read on . . .

▶ ⑫ Turn right on Avenue O, a one-way street.

1902 Avenue O
This corner was the original site of Nettleton's home before it was moved back on the alley, leaving this corner empty. To save it from being demolished, this high-raised, single bay cottage, built in 1888 at 14th and The Strand, was moved here in 1983.

1928 Avenue O

Standing next to a dormered beach cottage built in 1889, this transitional Victorian featured a more horizontal then vertical orientation, accented by its double-gallery. Its gingerbread, however, is typical of the earlier style. Nathaniel A. Spence of the Texas Produce & Commission Company hired Donald N. McKenzie to build this house in 1906.

2009 Avenue O

Looking ahead to the next block, on your left, note the 1892 L-fronted tenant cottage. Dressmaker Tenie Dobbert moved here with her mother and brother the next year.

▶ **⓭ Turn right on 20th Street, then left on Avenue N½. Park on the right side of the street in front of the first house. Walk the next working-class neighborhood beginning down N½ to 21st Street.**

2002 Avenue N½

This folksy 1870 German carpenter cottage, sans porches, originally stood in the 3800 block of Broadway. Built for Louis Wenzel, a bookkeeper for H. Marwitz and Company, it was moved to this location circa 2003 to replace another house that had been badly damaged in a 1977 fire. Wenzel had sold his home on Broadway to another German immigrant, Rudolph Bullacher, the year after it was built. Over 85 years in the same family, it had housed twenty-two children. Its first restoration in 1979 by contractor W. G. Mayo revealed its three expansions over the years. The house that burned at this location had originally been built by Henry and Minnie Henck during the 1890s.

2008 Avenue N½

This Victorian features an Eastlake balustrade with a side porch. The Hencks had also built this raised three-bay cottage in 1893 as a rental, but he moved his own family here five years later. It remained in the family until 1974.

2018 Avenue N½

Built in 1886, this single story cottage was enlarged during the early 1890s. Note its paired Ionic columns and walk-through windows.

2019 Avenue N½

Across the avenue, this wing of the larger Albertson house next door featured three columns with subtle Italianate elements but with a newer Arts and Craft front door. A series of tenants had left it in deplorable shape, but it was restored as a single-family dwelling circa 2004.

2017 Avenue N½

Next door, cotton-classer turned cotton-buyer Charles Muckle's company built this Greek Revival Southern townhouse with four octagonal columns and bracketed eaves circa 1870.

2011 Avenue N½

As you walk across the avenue, you'll see a simple one-story cottage, built around 1875. Note one of the reconstructed Rosenberg Fountains in the San Jacinto Community Garden next door.

▶ **Now, walk east to 20th Street and turn left, going north.**

1513 20th Street

Self-taught gardener and horticulturist Henry Stringfellow built this small shotgun house in 1867. The following year, he sold it to Mrs. Elizabeth Spencer, who had it moved fifteen feet to the north to make way for the Henck Cottage. Stringfellow moved to Hitchcock to cultivate a pear and Satsuma orange orchard, but moved back to 1407 Ball to write his book, *The New Horticulture*, in 1896 (see the walking guide).

1509 20th Street

In December 1903, Frank Schorer, a dealer in firearms, fishing tackle and sporting goods, built this raised Queen Anne cottage, with a gabled bay on its north side. Two years later, records show his widow Marie living here alone until 1909 when gunsmith Victor Schorer moved in—rather his brother, nephew, son, or her paramour is unclear. In 1923 the widow sold it to stenographer William S. and Essye K. Pask. After it had been abandoned for eight years, new owners bought the "working man's house" in 2001 and restored it.

▶ **⑭ Retrace your steps back to your car. Driving again, turn right on 21st Street.**

1527 21st Street
Punctuating the avenue directly in front of you sits an 1896 side entrance home with double galleries and a gable.

1522 21st Street
This five-bay-wide suburban villa, built by Frederick W. Muller in 1885, featured a centered dormer, floor-length shuttered windows and side gables.

1502 21st Street
Typical of family-owned corner stores of its time, the second story of this 1885 building served as the family living quarters of owner Arend H. Schutte. In addition to selling groceries, dry goods and beer, he and his partner Hermann Kuhnmann made flavorings and extracts. Featured on the 2006 Historic Homes Tour, the store was encircled by a canopy which was extended to a one-story addition to the south built in 1948.

▶ **⑮ Turn left on Avenue N.**

2115 Avenue N
Widow Mrs. Madeline Fivel built this raised, side-gabled house in 1891. Note the gingerbread on its small front porch. Other Fivel family members lived on the block, perhaps in the similar **2119 Avenue N**, which predated the widow's home by ten years.

2214 Avenue N
This coastal cottage was built in 1918.

1502-1504 Tremont

Built in 1913, this two-story frame home featured a west-facing sleeping porch with porte cochere on its south side. Dr. M. M. Mihovil bought it from its fourth owner in 1930 and converted the first floor into a "sanitarium" for his chiropractic clinic. The second floor housed living quarters for his family and his mother, Mrs. Josephine Mihovil.

To the south next door at **1508 Tremont** stands the Martin P. Morrissey house, built in 1897 by this imported building materials merchant. Although it bears a striking resemblance to homes designed by N. J. Clayton, no documents list him as the architect. You will find the mid-block Elks Lodge in the walking guide.

1504 23rd Street (aka Tremont)

▶ ⑯Turn right on 23rd Street, aka Tremont.

During the city's early years, Tremont Street was the most fashionable residential avenue. After the Civil War, this street became ripe for commercial development as Broadway became the boulevard for Galveston's grand mansions.

1424 Tremont

The Mission-style Silberman Apartments were designed by architects Green and Finger in 1913. A ground-level storefront was added in 1957.

1403 Tremont

Across the street, educator James M. Findley and his wife Jessie built this Queen Anne cottage in 1885 as rental property. He added a wing to the five-room cottage in 1906 and finally sold it to widow Mrs. Anna T. Smith in 1942. Twenty years later, George E. Quebe bought the house and it remained in that family for forty years.

1320 Tremont

This block once housed the substantial historic homes of Thomas M. League and lawyer-turned-judge John W. Harris. Constructed circa 1858-59, the three-story, Greek Revival League house served as a prominent hotel and boarding house under the ownership of Col. J. D. Waters right after the Civil War. In 1927 the Catholic diocese purchased it from then-owner Col. W. L. Moody, Sr., as well as the 1890 brick Clayton design belonging to Judge Harris next door to be used as their boys' high school. Both were demolished in 1941 to make way for a modern school, which opened one year later. Designed by architect Raymond Rapp, note the name Kirwin inscribed in the limestone entry above the door. Eventually, the gym and cafeteria, built exactly twenty years later and also designed by Rapp, were built on the corner where the League/Moody home had originally stood.

Across the street, the stylized **Pennington Buick** was built in 1951 at **1303-09 Tremont**. Mr. E. J. Pennington, Sr., had bought out the previous Buick dealer in town, who was located just two blocks down the street on 23rd, eight years earlier. He hired architect Ben Milam to design and build this functional, concrete structure which replaced the William McVitie "Gay '90s" Victorian home. Celebrating its Grand Opening on December 3, 1951, his new air conditioned showroom was crowned by the maroon and blue Buick logo; now, t-shirts are silk-screened here.

2314 Avenue M

When you stop at the intersection of 23rd and Avenue M, look to your left and down the block to note this classic wood-frame Greek Revival. Built in 1866 by coffee importer Charles Adams, this large two-story home originally stood on the corner of Avenue M, facing Tremont Street. In 1921 it was moved to the middle of the block and rotated to face the avenue to allow for further commercial development along 23rd Street.

▶ **Continue driving north on Tremont to Broadway.**

2302 Avenue L

One block to the north stands the Mott house. Born in Alexandria, Louisiana in 1837, Marcus Fulton Mott moved to Galveston with his parents eight years later, where he grew to become a respected lawyer at the oldest continuous law firm

23rd and Ave L

west of the Mississippi. A colonel during the Civil War, he was nicknamed "The Captain" when he helped to establish the Galveston Artillery Club. He built this home in 1884 and, although he died in 1906, "The Captain" is still said to be in residence . . . perhaps that's why the current owner chose to paint the house and its adjoining retail shops red!

1103 Tremont

A telegraph operator, George C. Smith built this 25-room boarding house in 1913. Designed by his wife, the three-story building featured electric call bells and speaking tubes. Note its impressive mansard roof.

This ends your exploration of Galveston's Victorian east end, both north and south of Broadway.

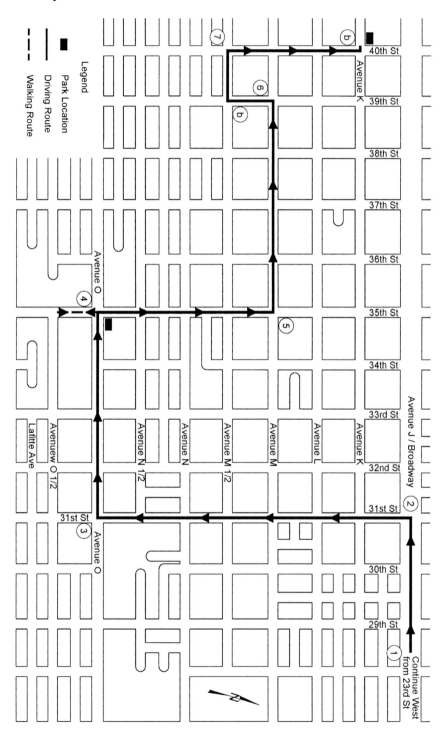

CHAPTER 5

Meandering Through Mid-Town to Walk the Broadway Cemetery

▶ **❶ From 23rd or Tremont Street, turn left on Broadway.**

You could continue driving west on Broadway, and turn left on 40th Street then right into the Cemetery—**OR you could follow the more rambling, scenic route below.** Even if you separate the two areas in this chapter, please do not miss the 35th Street mansions, Avenue O apartments and house!

3022 Broadway

Galveston architect, Raymond Rapp, traveled the United States studying the architecture and construction of funeral parlors before designing this facility for Frank P. Malloy. Taking four years to build, the Malloy and Sons Funeral Home opened on August 16, 1930, as "the South's finest funeral establishment."

▶ **❷ Turn left on 31st Street**

3100 Block of Avenue K

At the intersection, look to your right. The houses on this block typify a working-class neighborhood in the Old Central area, where most of the minority factory workers lived. Some speculate that these wooden Gulf Coast cottages date to just after the Civil War but the exact construction years are unknown.

1326 31st Street

In 1930, engineer Andrew Fraser designed this brick-faced industrial building with Art Deco detail to house the Rex Steam Laundry, owned by W. L., Jr., and his son Shearn Moody.

1420 31st Street

In 1886 Bishop Nicholas Gallagher established the first African American Catholic School in the state, located in the East End south of Broadway at 12th Street and Avenue K. The Dominican Sisters so increased its enrollment that a larger building had to be constructed. Three years later, a new "industrial school" with four classrooms was built further west at 25th and Avenue L, specializing in the "domestic arts." Officially sanctioned as Holy Rosary, a church was added to the complex and Father Phillip Keller from Germany became its first pastor. All of the parish buildings were moved to this present location in 1914, when a high school curriculum was incorporated. In 1927, Holy Rosary became the first accredited Catholic high school for African-Americans in the state. It continued in operation until 1941; a second school operated here from 1953 to 1979. The present church opened in April 1950. Partially destroyed by fire on New Year's Eve 1975, repairs were completed by Easter the next year.

1504 31st Street

George B. Stowe designed this Victorian home for railroad executive Lucius J. Polk in 1899. Note the original water cistern in the back.

1505-17 31st Street

Observe the group of red brick buildings on your right. On January 1, 1937, Carlos Ippolito bought this property from Ida M. Gross, specifically "in Mullers special subdivision of the east half of the northeast quarter of lot 38." Over the course of ten years, he constructed the buildings to house his Dr. Pepper Bottling Plant. He sold it to O. C. Unbehagen in 1964, who held the land and improvements until 1975.

▶ ❸ Turn right on the one-way Avenue O.

You will find the homes to the left in the walking guide.

3102 Avenue O

Behind a tall chain-link fence sits the exclusive Galveston Artillery Club. Originally chartered in 1841 to protect the port and city, it was reorganized as the city's most prestigious social club in 1899. Until 1955 its clubhouse stood at 19th and Seawall, when this modern mid-century structure, designed by Thomas M. Price, was built.

3111 Avenue O

Young attorney Adrian Levy built this imposing stucco house, with its curved driveway up to the front door, in 1922. Serving as mayor from 1935 to 1939, he hosted Franklin D. Roosevelt in 1937, introducing the President to a young, up-and-coming politician, Lyndon B. Johnson. As guests of Capt. Eddie Ricken-backer, Levy and his wife Pearl traveled to New York on August 4, 1938, to attend a ticker-tape parade honoring a former "BOI" Douglas "Wrong Way" Corrigan's return from Dublin, Ireland. Not to be outdone by the "Big Apple," Mayor Levy organized Galveston's own celebration of the confused pilot 22 days later (see the next chapter). The City Council proclaimed May 23, 1967, "Adrian Levy, Sr., Day" to honor the mayor and his wife.

3121 Avenue O

Next door, this classic Southern townhouse was built in 1872 by B. F. Hutches, a teller at the First National Bank of Galveston. Originally standing on the western half of three quarters of an acre lot, this two-story home features a single-bay columned entry and door with diamond sidelights, windows and transom, which were added in 1912.

▶ Continue driving west on Avenue O, moving to the right lane before 35th Street. Depending upon the time of day, this street can be busy!

3315 Avenue O

Two blocks farther west marked by a porte cochere on its right side, you will find the family home of Oscar Hoecker, "Born On the Island" in 1855. An official public cotton-weigher for the State of Texas, he built this traditional American Craftsman home in 1916 for wife Laurence, born in New Iberia, Louisiana, of French-speaking parents, and their family of twelve. Note its horizontal orientation, central gable supported by exposed rafters and squared porch posts—typical of Frank Lloyd Wright's Prairie style structures.

3320 Avenue O

On the north side of the street, lawyer John Charles Harris built this Victorian cottage in 1891. Born in New York in 1860, he came to Galveston after he married Florence Homland Parlow in 1886 and opened a law firm with his brother Edward. After the 1900 Storm, they moved to Houston and, after repairs were made, rented this cottage out until they sold it in 1920 to real estate agent Clarence Hervey. Practically destroyed by fire in 2005, the Galveston Historical Foundation rescued it to restore, and make it a model for the environmentally friendly Green Revival houses.

3328 Avenue O at the corner

Nine years after the Great Storm, Edwin D. Chadick and his wife Rosa signed a contract with Dupree and Gracey for improvements to this house which was originally built for Joseph P. Day the year before. Both were railroad men—Day worked for Galveston, Houston & Henderson while Chadick worked for the Katy Railroad (Missouri, Kansas and Texas). This grand dollhouse of a home, described as Queen Anne with Colonial Revival elements, featured ionic columns, a wrap-around porch and a tower. A succession of owners followed over the years until the house was restored in 2000.

3401 Avenue O

This home was built in 1909 for Alfred C. Torbert, who worked for the Gulf, Colorado & Santa Fe Railway.

▶ ❹ Turn right on 35th Street. Park your car and walk across the avenue to explore the varied structures down 35th Street.

3427 Avenue O

Built in 1847 as a private home and guest house, the Greek Revival Powhattan House originally stood between 21st and 22nd Streets and Avenues M and N, in the East End and south of Broadway. In 1893 the estate of Henry Rosenberg funded a new orphanage on that site, which threatened this residence of John Seabrook Sydnor, an early Galveston mayor, commodities merchant and slave trader.

Magnolia Sealy's sister, Caroline Willis Ladd, bought the

3427 Ave O

house and had it moved to this outlot at 35th and Ave O, which had been deeded to her by her husband, "for use as her own." British W. H. Tyndall supervised the move, separating the house into three two-story wings. He placed the central section of the original house on this corner, complete with its dramatic 24-foot Doric columns constructed of white virgin pine from Maine. Tyndall then added a second wing to its west side, but that made the house encroach on 35th Street. That wing was moved to its east side and used as rental property before it was destroyed in a fire. The third wing can be seen five blocks south at **2222 35th Street**, easily recognized by its matching columns. Here, Mrs. Ladd's "small country place" has served as the home of the Galveston Garden Club since 1965, which restored it twenty years later.

1718 35th Street

Behind the Sydnor home, banker Robert K. Hutchings and his wife Drusilla built this French Eclectic manor house in 1934. "B.O.I." architect Donald Barthelme designed this romantic revival, his only house in Galveston. Moving to Houston to work for John Staub, he became nationally recognized for his practical modernistic designs.

1718 35th Street

1804 35th Street

In contrast, George B. Stowe designed this Victorian home on the corner for dry goods merchant Felix E. Mistrot in 1899.

▶ **Cross the Street**

1715 35th Street

Born in 1882, Hans Guldman of Denmark and his wife, Marguerite, moved to Galveston from New Orleans in 1907. Serving as the city's Danish Consul, he became an influential businessman and civic leader. In 1913, he started building a house on this outlot. After another horrible hurricane two years later, Guldman tore down that undamaged, unfinished structure, replacing it with this more substantial red brick Prairie style. Deemed more suitable for lavish entertaining, their outstanding home was surrounded by large formal gardens that featured a greenhouse, a pond with a fountain, kennels, and an

1715 35th Street

arbor overflowing with grapes, from which Marguerite blended wine. Hans died tragically while cleaning his pistol on August 1, 1932, at age 50; his wife lived in the home until her death in 1976.

1705 35th Street

On the southwest corner stands the Windsor Court Apartments. In 1937, neighbor Marguerite Guldman commissioned Cameron Fairchild of Houston to design this modern eight-unit complex for rental income. Glass blocks mark the interior stairwells.

3518 Avenue O

Across the avenue, note this quaint late Victorian raised cottage. Built in 1897 for Capt. George Wilson, it became the home of Miss Matilda "Molly" Walters after this most successful Postoffice Street madam retired in 1906.

1705 35th Street

▶ ❺ **Walking back to your car, drive north on 35th Street; turn left on Avenue M**

3517 Avenue M

Edward T. Austin, the cousin of Stephen F. who was known as the "Father of Texas," built this Greek Revival cottage for his new bride Marie Estelle Hebert in 1857 in the city's rural area. By 1868, he'd moved away from the farm to a plantation-style home at 1502 Market (see *Walking Historic Galveston*), leaving this cottage to change hands many times. Raised four feet in 1906, the home became the property of Harry and Caroline Garrett in 1939, remaining in the family for the next forty years.

3518 Avenue M

Across the street, carpenter and "cistern maker" Robert G. Garnett built this Italianate in 1878. Note its ornate brackets and unique bays, one in front with a side bay in the back on its east side. Garnett moved to Hitchcock in 1899 and sold the house to E. J. Biering. Five years later, freight agent E. K. Nichols bought the house and converted a shuttered back porch into a kitchen during the 1920s. It was originally restored in 1975.

3627 Avenue M

In 1880, Henry Eimar built a small, one-story home next door at **3625**. Twelve years later, Eimar's family moved up into this 1892 raised Victorian craftsman cottage, typical of middle-class homes of the era. This home featured much attention to small details in its central front porch, supported by turned columns, centered below two shuttered dormer windows on its top floor and its western bay. Insurance appraisers claimed that it survived the 1900 Storm because it was "constructed of Express lumber" from Tyler County, first brought to Galveston after the Great Fire of 1885. One of several painters and paper hangers in this area, Eimar rented out his original 1880 home, which the current owners tore down to add an extensive garden to the restored cottage.

3702 Avenue M

Catty-cornered across the street, Confederate Civil War veteran

Walter C. Ansell built this classic Gulf Coast cottage in 1871 for his new wife, Caroline "Lina" Schadt. Born in Germany, she immigrated to Galveston with her family in 1846, where she and her two brothers were orphaned during a yellow fever epidemic. Ambrose Crane, her future husband's uncle, adopted the children. In 1871, the same year of their marriage, Ansell established the Texas Ice Company, shipping ice from Maine and Massachusetts to Texas. The house to its west was originally a rear addition, but son Wallace moved it in 1916. Note its twin dormers and a separate side entry. The property stayed in the family until 1960, passing from one generation to another.

3810 and 3812 Avenue M

These two raised cottages were designed by N. J. Clayton in 1896 as tenant property for Adolf Kruger.

▶ ❻ **Turn right on 39th Street, then right on Avenue M½.**

3918 Avenue M½

Truly a hidden historical treasure at the city's most western edge, this raised cottage was designed by Nicholas Clayton in 1896 for meat market owner, Leopold Biehler. Its horizontal orientation featured a study in contrasts: rounded with squared and extension with recess—just within its front profile! While its porch wrapped around on its west side, a separate side porch deep-set on its east side offered a view of its garden— away from the nearby cemetery.

▶ ❼ **Turn right on 40th Street, then left into the Cemetery. Park on the north side of the driveway, next to the oldest cemetery, Old City to the right, bordered by Broadway.**

This chapter culminates in a walk through the Broadway Cemeteries. Subchapters for each of the seven list names of those respected and prominent individuals buried here for walkers to look for, most from this book but a few from the walking guide. As you wander this hallowed ground, see if you

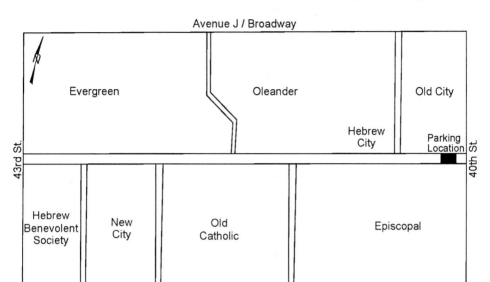

can discover your own "buried treasure" (pun intended) of other notables lying here.

Most of this information comes from records in Galveston/ Texas History Center on the third floor of Rosenberg Library, painstakingly transcribed by Doug and Linda McBee ("THE Cemetery Lady" on the Island) from the city's internment records, as well as from notes based upon their research on various war dead over the years. The stories she tells are amazing! Hopefully, a more complete and comprehensive book of all Galveston cemeteries will be forthcoming from this most passionate and knowledgeable pair!

Background History

The Galveston City Company donated four of these six city blocks as a public burial ground in 1840. They were divided into four burial grounds: Episcopal, Catholic, Old City and Old Potter's Field for the indigent.

John Groesbeck's revised city plan mapped the series of cemeteries with paved sidewalks and right-angled grids, edged by concrete curbs. As the city grew, so did its cemetery, with additions in 1864 and 1926. The original streets between the blocks were incorporated as burial grounds, which served as the final resting place of many of the Galveston's Founding Fathers. In addition, there is much speculation that there were many "two and possibly three-tier burial levels;" i.e., bodies buried on top of others' graves.

Elite Victorians marked their earthly lives with fancy headstones, monuments, vaults, and mausoleums. While some of those were imported from Germany, others were created by local architects. Whatever their origin, the installation of most Victorian markers in the Broadway cemeteries was administered by Charles S. Ott of the Monument Works bearing his name. Many of the more outstanding are included in this text.

In all, a total of 2,678 names can be found on tombstones and in records of those buried in these Broadway Cemeteries. Another noteworthy fact: sixteen Texas towns were named after people who were interred here. Most of them can either be located by a large grey granite monument erected by the State of Texas in 1936, or a plaque from the Texas Historical Commission.

After the 1900 Storm, two subsequent grade raisings, one in 1910 and the second in 1926, buried many of the oldest graves. Those lost graves included the first burial recorded, Emily Reed who died on November 22, 1841, at the age of 19, as well as that of Susan Dickerson, the "Babe of the Alamo" who ended her young life as a Galveston prostitute. Both were located in the original Old Potters Field for the poor and blacks that evolved into **Oleander Cemetery** adjacent to the first you'll walk. You will find the Malloy Vault here, for that family of morticians.

Old City Cemetery

Stepping out of your car to your right, you can explore some of the oldest graves, with their weathered and broken headstones here.

Closer to and facing Broadway on the left stands one of the cemetery's most memorable marble monuments, that of a pensive kneeling woman that honors John Reymershoffer and, on the other side of the path a little further south, a simpler stone marking his brother Gustav's family. They established the

Texas Star Flour Mill in 1876 at 21st and Avenue A (now called Harborside, see Chapter 1)—the city's largest individual success of the industrial era. Nearby stands the white mausoleum of J. P. Davie who established a trust fund for needy citizens.

William Harrison Sanduskey, who first mapped the City of Galveston in 1845, is buried in this section, as well as Henry Henck. His family built many rental cottages in the East End, both south and north of Broadway over the generations. Architect Donald McKenzie designed a large gray granite monument for his mother's—Justine Illies—grave in 1917; he and his half-brother were also buried here.

One of those Texas historical monuments marks the grave of a War of 1812 veteran. David E. Ayers, who came to the state in 1833 to sell Bibles, left the Alamo with William B. Travis'

The John Reymershoffer Monument

son. The two "led many families to safety during the Runaway Scrape." (Thanks, Linda!) A gray granite monument erected by the state during its centennial in 1936 marks the final resting place of Wilbur Cherry. After fighting for Texas during its War for Independence from Mexico, this New York-born patriot bought the *Galveston Weekly News* in 1843 from Samuel Bangs. At the time of his death 30 years later, he was still working there—as a printer.

Judge Johns Harris lies in **Old City Cemetery** alongside many of his family members, as well as George Ball, benefactor of the city's first public high school. The man who built "the most unusual house on an Island of unusual houses," John Clement Trube, born in Denmark, found his final resting place here, also with his progeny. The grave of Waters Davis, who brought the American National Red Cross to Galveston, is located in this section as well as those of the middle-class Ostermayer family from "Down the Island."

Note that a small number of early Jewish burials in the original **Hebrew City** are within this section, as they were not granted their own block until 1852. You will amble your way through that **Hebrew Benevolent Society**, on the 43rd Street side, later.

Across the driveway you will find two of the original cemeteries: Episcopal and Old Catholic bordered by Avenue L.

Most of the city's prominent founding fathers lie in the **Episcopal Cemetery**, bordering 40th and Avenue L. Galveston's first mayor, Major John Allen, is buried in this section close to the entrance in the center. Close by is another state monument dedicated to George Childress, who helped write the Texan Declaration of Independence. A business failure, he committed suicide in 1841 and his body was actually buried on the site of the original Rosenberg Elementary School. The daughter of Col. James W. Fannin, who fought in the Battle of Goliad, found her final resting place at the corner of 40th and Avenue L in 1849—Missouri Pinckney Fannin.

Major General John Bankhead Magruder of Virginia graduated from the U.S. Military Academy but joined the Confederates in 1861. He led their victory during the Battle of Galveston, fought on January 1, 1863. Although he died a pauper in Houston in 1871, the citizens of the Island city brought his body back here, marked by a tall spire that features carved battlefield images. Two monuments also stand in this section in tribute to those who fought and died during that battle, one for the Rebels, the other for the Yanks.

Businessman/banker Samuel May Williams and his young son Sam Jr. lay in this cemetery. Colonial secretary and chief financial officer to Stephen F. Austin during Texas' war of independence, he brought his pre-fabricated home at 3601 Bernardo de Galvez (aka Avenue P) from Rhode Island (see Chapter 8). The Browns of Ashton Villa have their family plot in this section, as well as the monuments of "Capt." Marcus Fulton Mott, who served as executor of Henry Rosenberg's estate and an investor in the Nottingham Lace Factory (see Chapter 7).

Magnolia Willis Sealy employed their Open Gates architectural firm of McKim, Mead and White to fashion a tall, pink marble monument for her husband George in 1903. She is also buried here as well as several of her children. You will find two Willis Vaults in this section—an ornate High Victorian crypt for Short A. and another for merchant P. J. Captain Henry Austin, a first cousin to Stephen F., is buried in the southwest corner; he came to Texas aboard the first steamboat in 1830.

Old Catholic

With a white altar centered on the Avenue L side, this cemetery lies between that of other Gentiles and the Jews. The most distinguished citizen buried in this section is Galveston's French Canadian founder, Michel Menard. You will find his grave toward the back on the east side.

Catholics of all classes rest in peace in this section of the Broadway cemetery. Self-proclaimed "Lord of Church Avenue," James Waters is buried here as well as ship Captain Joseph Boddeker, who fought for the Texas Navy during the Battle of Galveston.

As you wander the paths of this cemetery, look for a double headstone with photographs of two young World War II sailors. Tony and Frank Perugini, born on the same day two years apart, enlisted in the Navy while they were living in separate states.

Stationed on the cruiser, *New Orleans*, they were both in the same gun turret when the ship was torpedoed during the Battle of the Solomon Islands. Both lost their lives on November 30, 1942, and their story is chronicled in both this cemetery and Calvary Catholic on 61st Street.

Back in the cemetery, Michael Cahill donated Block 102 in 1841 to use for Yellow Fever victims. During the Civil War, both Rebels and Yanks who succumbed to the mosquito-borne disease were buried here. The New Cahill and Yellow Fever cemeteries combined to became **New City Cemetery**.

Even though most of the Hencks are buried in Old City, the granddaddy of them all, August, lies in this cemetery. Successful store merchants, the Genglers, have their family plot in this cemetery as well as dancing school instructor, Leona Lucille "Nonie" Mellen.

This cemetery serves as the final resting place for a very different family tragedy. Butcher Louis G. Alberti and his wife, Lizzie, were the proud parents of eight healthy children at the beginning of the "Gay '90s." Unfortunately, two of them succumbed to natural causes in 1894. Then, mysteriously four more Alberti siblings died on December 4 of that year, poisoned at the hands of their mother. Declared insane eight days later, she spent the remainder of her life in a San Antonio asylum. When Lizzie died of a morphine overdose in 1898, she was buried next to the children she had poisoned.

4109 Avenue L

Beyond the cemetery fence on the corner stands the Saints Constantine and Helen Serbian Orthodox Church. Established on January 13, 1895, the Slavonic parish bought this property within the year and constructed the oldest Eastern Orthodox Church in Texas and the second oldest in the United States. Two months later, the Very Reverend Theoclitos Triantafilides, became its first parish priest. A priest of the highest order at his death in 1916, Father Theoclitos was buried beneath the church's altar. He had studied and taught at several theological seminaries in Russia and was decorated twice by Czar Nicholas II, whose family became great benefactors of this Galveston church. Although rather plain-looking on the outside, this sanctuary houses many beautiful icons.

Hebrew Benevolent Society

Bordered by 43rd Street and Avenue L, this Jewish cemetery was not platted until 1853 as the city's large and growing Jewish population demanded and it was enlarged fifteen years later. Among the city's successful Jewish citizens buried here include merchant Leon and Henrietta Blum, whose High Victorian Gothic spire is truly outstanding. You'll also find families of Kempners and the Levys. Moritz Kopperl's elaborate marble marker, topped by a winged angel overlooking the graves, features relief portraits of the interred. Two unrelated Cohen families are buried in this section: retail businessman Robert I. and his wife Agnes Lord lie beneath a rectangular granite tombstone flanked by shell-like ovals. Closest to the central path you'll find Rabbi Henry with his wife Molly Levy who predeceased him.

Evergreen

Across the driveway on the north side and extending to the corner of 43rd and Broadway lies Evergreen, which was formerly Cahill. This egalitarian cemetery contains the graves of all classes of Galveston's citizens. From the wealthy to the commoners—the Harrells and a Stechmann—found their final resting places in this section. One of the former is signified by the John Sealy obelisk, designed by N. J. Clayton in 1885—one of the tallest in the city cemeteries. After his family established a bank—Ball, Hutchings and Sealy, his personal estate founded a teaching hospital that became the University of Texas Medical Branch in 1891.

Two noteworthy monuments stand near the Sealy marker. The first is a very ornate 1883 High Victorian monument of weathered white marble and red granite marking the grave of a rather unknown Athen V. Pichard. The final resting place of Mrs. John Sealy's brother, merchant B. R. Davis, was marked by a woman standing atop an open columned pedestal.

Brother to Gail who developed the process for condensed milk, Thomas H. Borden died a pauper on the Island, with his refusals to patent his inventions. Lawyer William Pitt Ballinger defended the Island against the Mexicans in 1836 and was appointed a U.S. District Attorney in 1850. In 1891, his daughter, Betty, organized the Daughters of the Republic of Texas with her cousin, Hally Bryan, in their home's library at 29th and Avenue O½ (see Chaper 8).

The Trueheart family lays next to the Adriances, business partners in the oldest real estate brokerage west of the Mississippi in life. Jens and Maude Moller—she quite the little developer, building numerous tenant houses in the East End after the Great Fire of 1885—found their final resting places in this cemetery. A pretty sailing ship marble relief adorns Captain Rufus Jameson's grave. Captured by the Union while running their blockade of the port, he went to prison for three years, released to live less than a year in his new home at 15th and Church.

Feel free to linger as long as you like, searching for and noting other familiar names. Come back time and time again, especially in the spring when the yellow and brown flowers are in full bloom. When you are ready to leave, this will conclude your walk of the seven Broadway cemeteries in Chapter 6 of *Beyond the Beaten Paths*.

CHAPTER 6

The City Spreads
West to the Airport

On the first anniversary of the catastrophic 1900 Storm, Galveston's city fathers pledged to build a concrete bulwark spanning the Gulf of Mexico to protect the barrier island against the initial full-force of tropical hurricanes. The first section of the Seawall was completed on the Island's southeast side from 6th to 23rd Streets in 1904. It gradually marched westward over the next 60 years to 103rd Street, making the Seawall a total of 10.4 miles long.

Standing behind the 17-foot-high breakwater, the Island city itself still remained at sea level—in effect, eye-to-eye with the warm Gulf waters. For further protection against in-land flooding, Alfred Noble, one of the three engineers who designed the Seawall, recommended raising the elevation of the city to the same level as its concrete bulwark, gradually sloping downward toward the bay to its north.

The New York firm of Goedhart and Bates devised the plan. Sand would be taken from the Port's channel using large self-loading hopper dredges, specially designed by Bates, which would then transport the murky muck via canal into one quarter-mile sections of the city. Pumped through pipes with such force, the stinky sludge spewed up, gushing high into the air. When the water

115

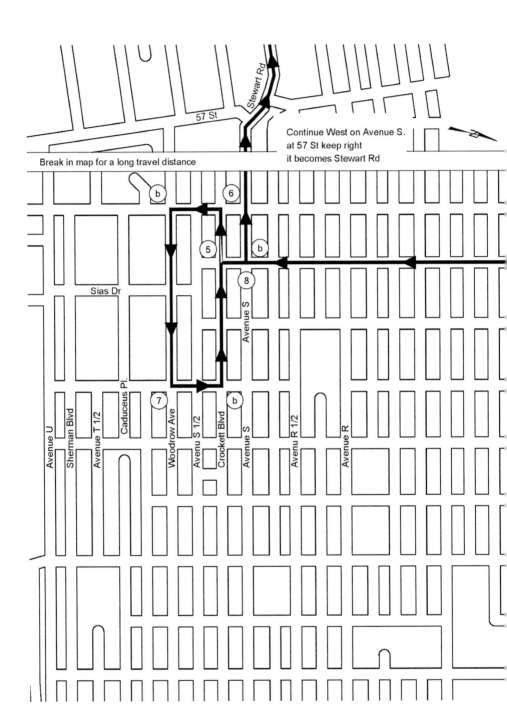

Continue West on Avenue S.
at 57 St keep right
it becomes Stewart Rd

Break in map for a long travel distance

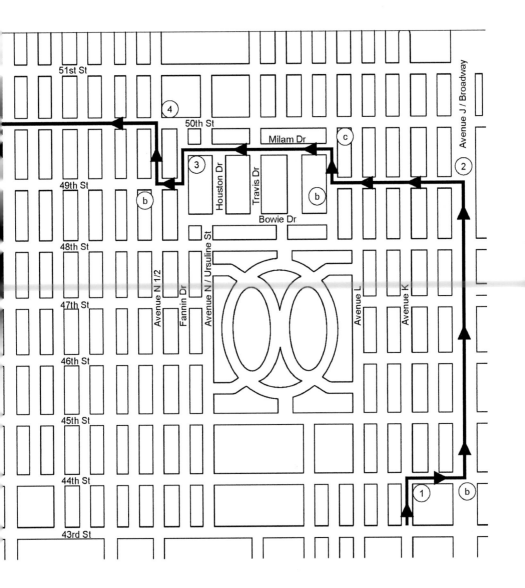

drained off and finally dried, the sand left behind would settle at a higher level. In essence, they proposed to raise the city by deepening the harbor! As many as eight dredges, all built in Germany, were employed in the initial east end project which took six years.

Within each section, individual homes were either jacked up on stilts to be filled underneath or sacrificed their above-ground, open basements to the muck. More than 2,000 stone structures, mostly churches, were raised by simultaneously moving hundreds of strategically-placed jackscrews to the beat of a drum, a ¼ inch at a time—at the owner's expense.

From 1905 to 1911, catwalks and trestles littered the city to provide walkways over the stinky sludge. After it finally dried, the elevation stood an average of eight feet above sea level. While the men paved the streets and lifted necessities like fire hydrants, trolley and train tracks, womens' groups completely replanted the new top soil on the newly-raised five hundred city blocks. Using tropical oleanders and south-hearty live oak trees, the ladies fully landscaped the city!

During its inaugural phase, Edmund Reed Cheeseborough served as secretary of the Grade Raising Board. From 1903 until 1926 when it was dissolved, this "rugged individualist" kept the project steadily moving forward toward completion through his tenacity. Indeed, many historians credit him with the success of this massive undertaking, although his name has been lost to obscurity. A small, slender and energetic man with piercing blue eyes, Cheesborough continued to walk to his downtown office from his house on 24th Street until he died in 1961 at the age of 93.

After the initial section of the city was successfully raised to 23rd Street, dredge operations followed the Seawall, moving westward, beginning in 1911. Broadway south to Avenue P from 33rd to 45th Streets was filled; five years later, those blocks immediately behind the Seawall had been lifted 21feet. In 1923, Galvestonians passed bonds of $1,250,000 to raise the area south of Avenue P to the Seawall and west to 53rd Street, with the westernmost areas filled in with the sludge from Offat's Bayou. This was completed under budget by Christmas Day 1925, hastening Galveston's westward expansion, particularly for suburban development.

A group of enterprising doctors led by Dr. Willard R. Cooke, lawyer Brantley Harris, and Judge Jules Damiani partnered to develop the north side of 45th to 47th Streets along Avenues T and

U, bordering the Fort Crocket artillery installation. Initially completed by October 1927, this subdivision was originally called Westmoor, but later became known as the Denver Court area. With Avenue S to its north and 53rd Street on its west, this area grew to more than 30 blocks in the three succeeding decades. While most of this neighborhood is covered in the walking guide, you will do a brief ride-through of Crocket and Woodrow Streets a little later in this chapter.

In July 1926 Clark W. Thompson joined his father-in-law, W. L. Moody III and Moody's father-in-law, W. D. Haden, to form the Cedar Lawn Development Company. Located between Avenues L and N, 45th to 48th Streets, this now gated community seems to "turn its back to the rest of Galveston" (or so wrote Beasley and Fox) as all of its homes face inward within nine square blocks re-platted into a butterfly pattern. Chapter 7 in *Walking Historic Galveston: A Guide to its Neighborhoods* thoroughly covers this lovely (and very elite) "Garden Spot."

In 1927 the company acquired an additional eight blocks adjacent to Cedar Lawn on its west side, slightly off-set from 48th to 50th streets and avenues L to N½. They called this modest middle-class development Palm Gardens and named its streets after Texas heroes. Lots were sold beginning in December and B. Wittjen started building small single-story homes the following year. By August 10, 1930, this "attractive residential center," already populated by 15 families, offered an "array of brick veneer bungalows" for sale.

▶ **❶ From the driveway within the cemetery, turn right on 43rd Street, then left on Broadway, traveling in the left lane.**

▶ **❷ Drive six blocks west, then turn left on 49th Street into the Palm Gardens development. Turn right on Austin and left on Milam; you will pass Wharton, Travis and Houston streets to your left.**

Although strictly middle-class, this suburban development featured its own set of Deed Restrictions. No businesses, especially those selling "spirituous liquors," could be located in

Entrance to Palm Gardens from 49th and Ave L

Palm Gardens, and only one residence could be built on each full-sized lot. No fenced yards in front, lawns had to be maintained, and no buildings could be moved into the new subdivision. Not only was keeping livestock prohibited, no house could "be sold, conveyed, leased or rented to any person or persons other than (those) of Caucasian race." Fortunately, these conditions expired on January 1, 1950.

▶ ❸ To exit Palm Gardens, turn left on Fannin, right on 49th then another right on Avenue N½.

▶ ❹ Turn left on 50th Street and drive south eight blocks across Avenue S to Crockett.

Developed with the automobile in mind, the Denver Court area started with one private dead-end street, Caduceus Place, in 1926. The subtle ½ block shift as well as its double length blocks caused regular city streets to dead-end at alleys or mid-block. Although little is known about the inside stories of these homes, a listing of addresses, architectural styles and years built was documented when the neighborhood association applied for official historical recognition from the state.

▶ ❺ **Turn right on Crockett Boulevard.**

This last block of the street has only three homes that maintain the overall historical integrity of the neighborhood: the 1941 Colonial Revival at **5005 Crockett**, the Tudor Revival built in 1941 at **5006** across the street and a Modern design circa 1945 at **5016**. The terms used to indicate a structure's historic significance within an area are either Contributing or Noncontributing.

5024 Crockett

Built in 1941, the authenticity of this traditional one-story home is obscured by its vinyl siding and modern oversized storm shutters. Therefore, it was deemed "Noncontributing."

▶ ❻ **Turn left on 51st Street; then another left on Woodrow.**

Note how the Denver Court street half melds into Avenue S½ at 51st Street. The houses in this block on Woodrow featured an eclectic mixture of styles through the decades of development. In this first block, note the 1941 Spanish style at **5028**, its Tudor Revival neighbor and, at **5022**, a 1929 Craftsman. On the south side of the street stands a Colonial Revival at **5027** built in 1940 and another Tudor Revival at **5009** built in 1938. Note there is no 4900 block.

Most of the houses in the next block contribute to the neighborhood's architectural integrity. They reflect primarily two styles, Modern and Tudor Revival that date from 1928 to 1948. As for those that are Noncontributing: **4815 Woodrow**, built circa 1965 and those whose restorations were less than period: **4806** and **4727**.

4816 Woodrow

The low-pitched-roof of this sprawling 1952 Ranch accents its horizontal orientation, broken only by its massive red Roman brick chimney, which also sharply contrasts its cream-colored façade.

As with the 5000 block, the 4700 block of Woodrow is a mixed bag, with many of the oldest Tudor Revival styles in this area, built from 1927 to 1939. Those homes listed as Contributing include two Craftsman designs, one at **4707** built in 1927 and **4720** built one year later. On the south side of the street, note in particular the 1928 Tudor Revival at **4715**, the Craftsman at **4709** built in 1930, and the Modern at **4705,** built five years later. The oldest home on this street stands at **4702 Woodrow**, a Modern house built in 1927.

▶ **⑦ Turn left on 47th Street and left again on Crocket.**

4804 Crockett Boulevard
Designed by Cameron Fairchild of Houston, this French Provincial "country house" sports an H-plan with two project- ing wings on its east and west sides. In place of a traditional

4804 Crockett

front porch, an arched trellis loggia spans the wings in its central section, topped with twin chimneys. Real Estate agent John Adriance II built the reddish pink brick house in 1929.

The final two blocks on your drive offers eclectic styles— Colonial Revival, Modern, and Tudor Revival with one of each a Prairie School/Mission built in 1929 at **4814 Crockett** and a 1933 Craftsman at **4828.**

▶ **❽ Turn right on 50th Street, then left on Avenue S. "The City Spreads West" travels to the airport next via Avenue S which becomes Stewart Road west of 57th Street.**

Crossing 61st Street, note the northwest corner, now a Chevron station. This was the original site of the Hollywood Dinner Club, built in 1926 for $50,000 in an ornate Spanish design. It was the first private supper club of its kind in the United States offering gourmet dining, drinking, dancing to top-name Hollywood entertainment and, if you knew who to ask, a little illegal gambling in its ultra private back room! Another first—it was air conditioned! Manager Sam Maceo gave the orders to keep the HDC cold enough "to keep 'em drinking and gambling!" Its first three weeks of operation saw 20,000 guests— most from *off* the Island—come through the doors and, within ten years, its reputation had spread nationwide via national

Hollywood Dinner Club, 61st and Stewart
—Courtesy of The Rosenberg Library, Galveston, Texas

radio live broadcasts. A young student newsman, in town covering another assignment, was asked to open one of those shows. With his distinctive voice, Walter Cronkite introduced Ben Bernie's band with, "Good Evening Everyone from Sam Maceo's Hollywood on the beach in Galveston." Unfortunately, the Texas Rangers closed the club down in 1939 with "planted narcotics," and the building languished as storage until a large fire on August 13, 1957, burned it to the ground.

▶ **9** When Stewart splits in two at 69th Street, continue driving straight, veering to the right onto Jones Drive. Turn right at the light on Hope Boulevard (the entrance to Moody Gardens), then a quick left on Airport Blvd.

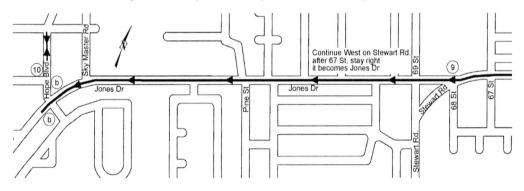

Entrance to Moody Gardens

▶ ⑩ **To explore Scholes International Field, turn right on Terminal Drive, then left.**

You'll discover that Galveston's airport is home to several helicopter companies that service the offshore oil industry

Aviation history began on Galveston Island as early as March 17, 1912, when Paul Studensky flew his Curtiss byplane onto

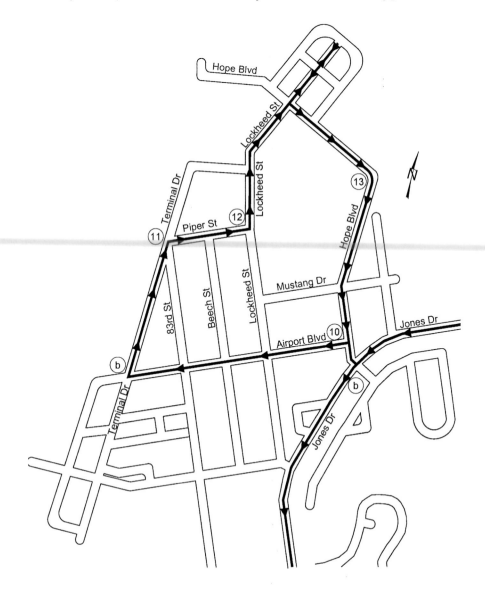

a field at 56th between Avenues Q and S to deliver "aeromail" from La Marque—the first recorded aerial postal delivery in the South. By February 6, 1928, this service had expanded to include other cities in the country with regular, twice-a-day service. Paul R. Braniff supplied the fleet of 18 planes. Along with the mail cargo, each could seat ten passengers, who usually traveled to the Island during summer.

On July 18, 1938, a Galvestonian flew into aviation history, albeit backwards. Born in a second floor apartment at the corner of 21st and Market on January 22, 1907, Clyde Groce Corrigan moved to Los Angeles with his mom and siblings after his parents divorced. Changing his first name to Douglas, he was hooked on flying in October 1925, after his first biplane ride.

He achieved his first solo flight within six months and became an airplane mechanic with Ryan Aeronautical Company in San Diego. That company won the bid to build Charles Lindbergh's "Spirit of St. Louis." **Douglas Corrigan** contributed an increase in the plane's lift by extending the wings ten feet. He bought a 1929 Curtiss Robin in 1933, damaged in a crash, to launch his own transatlantic flight to his beloved Ireland.

He modified the small plane, which he named "Sunshine," and applied to the Bureau of Air Commerce in 1935 for permission to fly across the Atlantic. This was denied many times and many more modifications later over the next two years, as his plane was declared as not being airworthy and grounded. In spite of this, Corrigan left Long Beach for Floyd Bennett Field in Brooklyn, New York, on July 9, where he filed his return trip to California for July 17. Manager Kenneth Behr cleared him to use any runway except the westernmost, which was positioned over the administration building, then wished him, "Bon Voyage!" Armed with a 20-year-old compass, water, two boxes of Fig Newtons—but no radio—he took off at 5:15 A.M., headed east . . . and never looked back.

Huddled behind a door tied shut with baling wire, Corrigan averted disaster twice during the flight when his "crate" filled with gasoline. After 28 hours and 13 minutes, he landed not in California but at Baldonnel Aerodrome in County Dublin. Insisting that it was a "navigational error" which he didn't realize until 26 hours into the flight, he had his pilot's license suspended for fourteen days—just long enough for both he and his "Sunshine" to sail back to the states on the steamship *Manhattan*. Arriving August 4, this maverick "Flying Irishman" was nicknamed "Wrong Way" Corrigan by the press and celebrated with ticker-tape parades in both New York and Chicago.

Not to be outdone in honoring a "Son of Treasure Island," Mayor Adrian Levy renamed the city's air field, Douglas Corrigan Airport, during a dedication ceremony on August 26. Landing his "crate" there that morning, the confused celebrity enjoyed a whirlwind "Welcome Home" that included the dedication with a parade from the city auditorium followed by a reception, where a local quartet crooned a parody of "Harrigan" replaced with Corrigan. His final stop was the Gill/League building where a bronze plaque at the entrance marked his birthplace. This building was demolished by the American National Insurance Company in July 1973 to build a parking lot for its new tower. Happily, "Wrong Way" would continue to capitalize on his mistake for the rest of his life!

Douglas "Wrong Way" Corrigan
—Courtesy of The Rosenberg Library, Galveston, Texas

With the advent of World War II, Corrigan's name disappeared from Galveston's airport when the War Department commandeered it in January 1941. As the Galveston Army Airfield under Major Henry C. Coles, three 6,000-foot-long hard surfaced runways were built for use in anti-submarine activities in the Gulf as well as for the Fort Crockett Artillery installation. Deactivated on November 15, 1945, the airport returned to civilian service again under the management of Robert H. Scholes, the only Galvestonian to own a private plane. Under his management, the Galveston Municipal Airport Terminal opened four years later closer to its present location.

To honor the man who had served as airport manager since 1932 with the exception of the war years, the city's municipal airport was renamed, Scholes Field on December 10, 1959. When he died at home of cancer the following June, airport commission chairman, Jimmy Phipps called him a brother who was "completely irreplaceable." That impossible task fell to John R. "Rusty" Mullins two short weeks later.

▶ ⑪ Turn left from the terminal driveway, then right on Piper (or enter the Lone Star Flight Museum parking lot and drive through.)

What started as a private aircraft collection in June 1985, found a home five years later at Scholes Field. The Lone Star Flight Museum, housed in a 50,000 square-foot facility, grew to become one of the finest collections of restored historically-significant aircraft in the country. Most of the forty+ vintage WWII Fighters, Bombers and Trainers on display still fly, such as a B17 Flying Fortress and a Grumman F4F Hellcat. In addition, you'll find an aviation library and over 1,500 artifacts and memorabilia on display in this non-profit, privately-funded museum. Since Hurricane Ike in September 2008, inflicted $20 million damage to its collection, the flight museum may be moved up to Ellington Field within the next five years.

▶ ⑫ Turn left on Lockheed.

Note Schlitterbahn Waterpark on the right side of the street (to the east).

▶ **Continue straight toward the Visitor's Center. With its entrance blocked to traffic, you will have to turn left in a "U-turn" to drive through the rest of the Moody Gardens complex. Note the pyramids to the left.**

Conceived in 1983, Moody Gardens began with a horse barn called Hope Arena that housed a hippotherapy program for those individuals with severe head injuries. That therapy expanded within three years to include animal and horticultural programs, employing those with other mental or physical disabilities. By 1986 the original riding arena had morphed into a convention center, while Palm Beach with its gleaming white sand barged in from Florida launched the lush, tropical gardens on its way to becoming a world-class tourist destination. This closed the therapy program. Today, this 242-acre of once undeveloped airport property features three pyramids: the environmentally sensitive Rainforest, a 1.5 million gallon Aquarium and the scientific-minded Discovery Pyramid with environmental and educational missions. You can also experience 3-D IMAX films and rides at the Visitors' Center. Completing the package, the Hotel/Spa opened in 1999, offering spectacular city views and, just for plain fun, Schlitterbahn Waterpark followed in Summer 2005.

▶ **⑬ Turn left onto Hope Boulevard. You'll see the hotel on the left and, behind it, the Convention Center. Exit the complex by turning right onto Jones Drive, which becomes 81st Street, driving south to Steward Road. Now you're ready to venture "Down the Island" in Chapter 7.**

Down the Island

▶ **❶ From 81st Street, turn right on Stewart Road, a twisty
rural trail with several sharp "Dead Man" curves.**

Think of a SSSSnake . . . and please watch your speed! Staying
on Stewart, you will pass many historic sites, until the street
eventually curves into 13 Mile Road which will take you to FM

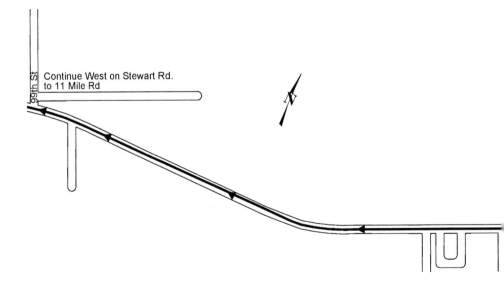

(Farm-to-Market) 3005. A note of caution: This road is currently undergoing a widening project that will last well into 2013. Please be aware that some addresses are not clearly marked and traffic delays are distinctly possible.

Just west of the southern border of the airport on your right stands the 75-acre tract called Campeche Cove, which the Sullivan family started developing in May 1976.

The west end of Galveston Island officially begins at the 8 Mile Road and ends at the San Luis Pass with a toll bridge to Freeport. Between these points, scattered houses, rustic camps and beach "stilt" houses sit among clusters of beach communities, on both the Bay (to the right) and beach sides. While some began as early as 1956, many more reflect the 1970s and '80s, with more lavish and opulent construction continuing to the present. Signs at 99th Street advertise the recently-remodeled Moody Gardens Golf Course (once known as the city-owned Municipal Golf Course or "Muni" for short) and Evia, another modern housing development that blends the new with elements of old Victorian. If you want to explore it, turn right— but this driving guide of historic Galveston will continue on Stewart Road.

As the city prospered, its citizens looked west for escapes from city life. In 1884 four of Galveston's most prominent cit-

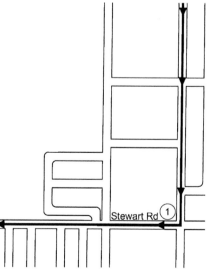

izens—Walter Gresham, H. A. Landes, W. L. Moody and Julius Runge—invested in a fledgling narrow-gauge railroad, the Galveston and Western Line. The first length of track laid was a thirteen-mile track from Pier 9 across the city to what would become Fort Crockett in 1897, then westward to 12 Mile Road. For more than fifteen years, it offered regularly scheduled Sunday outings from aboard its "Little Susie," named after the builder's daughter, to "excursionists" and by 1892, "an active suburb" had developed. Their rather grandiose plan for their railroad was to extend the line across the San Luis Pass through

Stewart Rd ①

Corpus Christi, and eventually connect the port city with the Valley. To the east, the partnership hoped to link it to New York via a transcontinental system. However, heavily damaged during the 1900 Storm, the little railway never got off the Island but instead hauled sand during the grade raising.

The foundations of a lace curtain factory lay south of Stewart Road ¼ mile east of 11 Mile Road and one mile east of Lake Como. In 1892 Raphael Behrens—an enterprising German— chose west Galveston Island to build his Nottingham Lace Company, with its proximity to state-grown cotton. In addition, the Island's humidity, which prevented the fabric from bunching together during the process, made its climate "superior to that of (cold and damp) Manchester, England." Behrens im-

Nottingham Lace Factory, between 11 and 12 Mile Road
—Courtesy of Kirk Clark

ported specialized machinery and experienced lace makers from the UK, staffing his new Texas company with young ladies whose small, dexterous hands suited the delicate craft. Three months after it was incorporated in May 1893, the factory was busy spinning out curtains to meet demands. The small colony of Nottingham grew rapidly with stores, a post office and school, residences and three beer saloons. However, according to research by historian Kirk Clark, the anti-European business policies of Governor Hogg caused Behrens to default on his start-up loans, forcing the factory into bankruptcy. By 1896 its highly sophisticated machinery was removed and what was left of the building was destroyed during the great storm four years later.

For the previous 500 years, West Galveston Island was Karankawa Indian territory. This amalgamation of four tribes with a common language and culture roamed the Texas Gulf coast from the Bay southwestward to Corpus Christi. They traveled the shallow waters in groups of 30 to 40 in dugout canoes, with domesticated canine companions, a coyote-like breed. The men, tall and muscular, were powerful runners who coated their bodies with a stinky mixture of either alligator or shark grease and dirt to ward off the blood-sucking mosquitoes. To celebrate their war victories, they engaged in ceremonial cannibalism, either as revenge or to capture their enemies' courage and power. Women of the tribe made pottery and wove baskets, which they lined with natural tar from the Gulf beaches.

Most of our knowledge of the Karankawa and other early Texas tribes came from the writings of Alvar Nunez Cabeza de Vaca who landed on the Island in 1528 with a crew of 49, including the darker-skinned slave Esteban who had a gift for languages. The Spaniards, from the ill-fated Narvarez expedition in Florida, stumbled upon an Indian campsite, protected by 200 warriors from several villages, armed with longbows. After an exchange of gifts, the Indians befriended, sheltered and nourished de Vaca's emaciated men. Despite the kindnesses, many succumbed to exposure or disease during the harsh winter, prompting them to call the island Malhado meaning "bad fortune"; by spring, they numbered fourteen. Most of the group moved westward and further diminished while their ailing leader recovered to become a trader among mainland tribes until he was enslaved.

Four Narvarez survivors reunited in 1535 to slip away from their Indian masters. Moving southwest toward Mexico, Esteban again led the group, easing communication. Gaining quite a reputation as shamans able to heal anyone of anything, the four arrived in Mexico City on July 23, 1536, as celebrities. With visions of the mythical "Seven Cities of Gold" dancing in his head, the Mexican viceroy named Mendoza detained them until they convinced him to buy Esteban as his guide. The three others sailed back to Spain the following year, where Cabeza de Vaca wrote an account of his travels in the New World from memory.

Fast-forward to 1784. Discovering that journal in the Spanish archives, Count Bernardo de Galvez commissioned a survey of the Island and its bay as a claim for Spain (see the walking guide). From 1817 to 1821, buccaneer Jean Lafitte moved his Louisiana pirate colony to Campeche on the east end of Galveston's natural port, where he ruled as the "Terror of the Gulf" from his Maison Rouge (see Chapter 1). Since captured slaves were prohibited from sailing into the harbor, Lafitte established another settlement in this area not only to serve as another point from which to prey upon unsuspecting ships, but also to unload their human cargo; the freebooters then marched their appropriated "property" into the city where slaves were sold for $1 per pound at one of its three auction blocks.

On the south side of Stewart (to your left) just before you reach 12 Mile Road, you will find a grey granite monument at the recently burned-out Lafitte's Grove. It was erected in tribute to the pirate king by the State of Texas upon its Centennial in 1936. If you choose to pull off for a closer look, be careful as rattlesnakes have been sighted coiled on its grounds.

At this location in February 1819, the pirates fought the Indians over a woman, called the Battle of Three Trees. Lafitte's men kidnapped a Karankawa maiden and the tribe wanted her back. Three hundred brave warriors attacked the settlement but their longbows were no match for the fort's two cannons. The few survivors fled to the San Antonio area where Spanish priests attempted to convert the tribe to Christianity. They eventually migrated to Mexico in 1844 to be absorbed into that culture. Legend has it that the spirit of the Indian maiden still wanders the area.

Continuing west on Stewart, you will pass another golf course on your right which is part of the private, "Members Only" Galveston Country Club at 1700 Sydnor Lane. Just past 12-Mile Road again to your right, the Waterman at Pirate's Cove recently reopened after Hurricane Ike. Thirteen years ago, this charming restaurant was constructed of 10,000 square feet of warm antique long leaf pine salvaged from cotton warehouses. Featuring spectacular sunset views over Galveston Bay, expansive outdoor docks and the freshest seafood, Waterman's is truly a unique dining escape on the Island! Next door stands the Stewart Mansion.

The Stewart Mansion

Although this house was not built until 1926, the property it sits on was the Island's highest elevation and development dates to 1831, as Warren D. C. Hall, Secretary of War during the state's War of Independence against Mexico, had a house here. In 1874, his widow sold the site to Capt. Marcus F. Mott who built his ranch "Alta Loma" on the shores of Lake Como. He used the two-story residence known as "Oak Bayou" as a weekend getaway, where he entertained Texas dignitaries with lavish parties. An investor in the lace factory, Mott intended to develop another city named "Mottexas" to replace Nottingham until he died on November 18, 1906. His daughter, Lillian Mott Cash, leased the property which included the land of the Galveston Country Club to Elmer Ellsworth Dana, the former manager of the lace factory.

This self-proclaimed "Mayor of Danaville" opened a boarding house with catering by a Mr. Armstrong, who quickly became famous for his oyster roasts and Sunday picnics. Stewart Road was built from the Seven Mile Post to 13 Mile Road sometime around 1913, but the only remnant of Nottingham was the colony's school. Henry Ostermayer's descendants continued to populate their birthplace through the mid-1950s, while the land was used for farming and cattle grazing.

After Dana's house was destroyed by fire 1925, the land sold to Eugenia Taylor and George Sealy. Their "Isla Ranch" weekend get-away was designed by San Antonio father/son architects Atlee and Robert Ayres. More of a "camp" than home, the original layout featured a large living room with a glassed-in front porch, two bedrooms with attached baths and a smaller room for bunk beds. The dining room, kitchen and breakfast pantry lead to a single row of wood-frame cottages for servants and guest log cabins. In 1933 Sealy traded "Isla Ranch" to Maco Stewart, Sr., for his property at 53rd and Seawall. The complex on Stewart Road passed to Maco Jr. five years later when his dad died.

He and his wife Virginia "Margie" Kirkland enlarged and air conditioned the main house in 1939-40. On the west side, they added a large master bedroom suite, its bath covered in mirrors that were painted with pink flamingos and water lilies. A library complete with motion picture equipment and a sun deck with a bed and bath for Mrs. Stewart's private maid filled the northwest corner with a three-car garage behind it. Margie had a pirate mural painted on the walls of the large living room, next to the dining room which stood to the east. An expanded concrete kitchen stood by the driveway with a two-apartment servant's quarters attached, making the house 7,000 square feet. A Spanish tiled walk with concrete arches, patio and fountain outside to the west connected with two large swimming pools. Completing the compound, renamed "Lazy S Ranch," was a concrete and tile fence along Stewart Road, with lights on each post and a large entrance arch that still reads "Stewart Mansion."

The couple entertained numerous guests and state dignitaries from January 1939 to 1945. During these parties, Margie fell in love with Lt. Mike O'Daniel, the son of Governor W. Lee "Pass the Biscuits, Pappy" O'Daniel. The couple divorced in October after she deeded her share of the property to her ex. The O'Daniels were married on January 19, 1946, just ten days after Stewart moved on with Virginia Beall, reportedly an airline pilot who played baseball in high heels. Their happiness was cut short, however, when Maco Jr. died of a heart attack on December 16, 1950, while driving home from a Christmas party at the Artillery Club. He was buried close to the house.

Just prior to their marriage go-rounds, Maco and Margie had donated their mansion to UTMB on June 23, 1944. It opened as the Margie B. Stewart Convalescent Home for Children on

February 12, 1946, with a full staff and six patients, although it was equipped to handle thirty. Since transport of children and supplies proved most difficult due to its distance from the hospital and the free-roaming livestock on the only paved road, the home closed on March 18, 1949. The hospital's Executive Director Dr. Chauncey D. Leake moved into the house, while Maco Jr.'s widow, Virginia, lived in one of the guest cottages until June 28, 1958, when she married Edmund F. Ball of Muncie, Indiana. The following year, 13 red granite markers were erected along Stewart Road beginning at 61st Street in memory of the Stewart family.

In his will, Stewart had stipulated that upon the deaths of his two sons, his "Lazy S Ranch" would be given to the state as Maco Stewart State Park. Either transferred or bought by the State Parks Bond Program in 1969, Galveston Island State Park opened in 1975 to campers and RV owners. Although tropical storms occasionally take their toll—especially Hurricane Ike— today, the park offers 180 Beachside and Bay side overnight camping sites priced at $5 a day, coastal prairie hiking, bird-watching, fishing and swimming on 1,998 acres.

▶ ❷ **Follow the curve where Stewart becomes 13 Mile Road.**

Around the curve off to the right you will see the ruins of the old Mary Moody Northen Amphitheater and cast apartments.

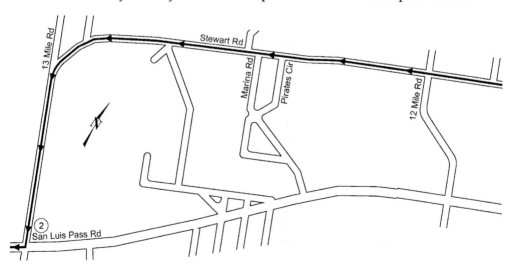

▶ Continue south to FM 3005 (Farm to Market Road) and turn right.

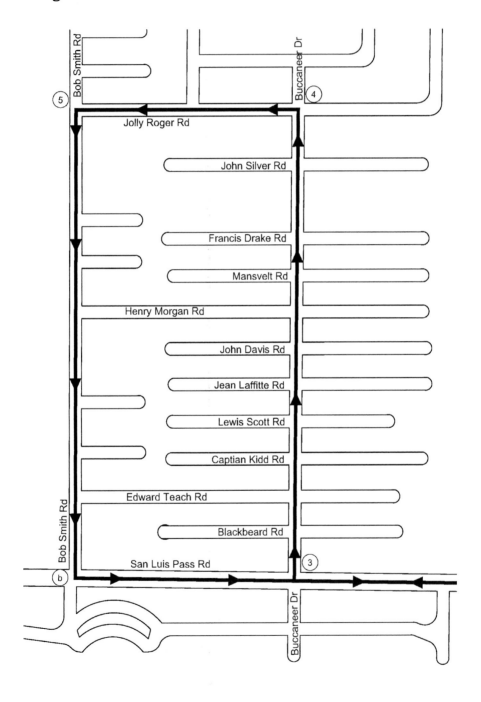

▶ ❸ When you reach Jamaica Beach, turn right at the light onto Buccaneer Dr.

▶ ❹ Toward the end, turn left on Jolly Roger Road. You'll find an open pavilion and park at the corner of Bob Smith Road and a Texas Historical Commission plaque honoring the Karankawas.

Once a weekend playground for tourists, this was the first community to develop down the Island after Hurricane Carla in 1961. While laying its infrastructure, bulldozers unearthed a Karankawan Indian campsite and burial grounds. To honor its hallowed ground, a below-ground display of artifacts and graves offered windows into the culture's spiritual life, with skeletons positioned exactly as they were found. The plaque was erected in 1966 to mark the display. Unfortunately, the exhibit was vandalized and removed from view. Although the founding corporation went

Jamaica Beach Historical Sales Piece
—Courtesy of Jack & Welcome Wilson,
Jamaica Beach Museum
via the City of Jamaica Beach

Karankawa skeleton, exactly as found
—Courtesy of Jack & Welcome Wilson,
Jamaica Beach Museum, in particular
cousins Cindi Proler & Kathlene Wilson

bankrupt during the early 1970s, the community moved forward and incorporated as the City of Jamaica Beach in 1975—complete with its own government, police and fire departments. The Indian bones were donated to the Texas Archeological Society, but the Indian artifacts and photos of the excavation and display case are maintained by the Jack and Welcome Wilson Jamaica Beach Museum.

▶ ❺ From Bob Smith Road turn left on FM 3005.

On the Gulf side to the right, note the stone canopies of the Galveston Island State Park beachside campgrounds.

On the other side of the road stands a most unusual residence that has been nicknamed the Kettle House. According to *Weird Texas* by Wesley Treat, it was built over fifty years ago by a man who used to construct oil storage tanks. Some think it resembles the top of an upside-down grain silo, and although it appears uninhabited, a man has been infrequently sighted making repairs.

After you drive through the large Pirate's Beach community, you'll see three of the four Pocket Parks at intervals on the right; the fourth is located way out west at 19 Mile Road. The County of Galveston owns numbers 1 and 3, while #2—known as Frank Carmona Park—is managed by the city's Park Board of Trustees. All offer restrooms, showers, concessions and picnic areas but there is no overnight camping.

Dellanera Park stands at 7 Mile Road on the beach side, a city-owned RV campsite. The pavilion at this year-round resort offers a gift shop, umbrella and chair rentals, showers and laundry facilities. Daily rates change with the season, ranging from $42 in the summer to a $20 off-season charge.

Note the Victoriana Beachtown and all the modern beach front condominium high rises just before you drive up onto the Seawall, thus ending your foray "Down the Island."

Campsite on the Gulf of Mexico
—Courtesy of Trey Goodman and Steve Alexander of the Galveston Island State Park

CHAPTER 8

... And Back Again

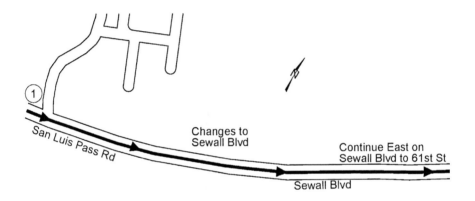

San Luis Pass Rd

Changes to
Sewall Blvd

Continue East on
Sewall Blvd to 61st St

Sewall Blvd

▶ ❶ **From the end of the Seawall at 103rd Street, continue to drive east.**

Note the various hotels, gas stations, apartments, cafes and condominiums that line your left side.

At 91st Street once stood Sea Arama Marineworld, one of the first ocean parks in the United States. Opened in 1965, the 25-acre attraction featured the Oceanarium containing a central 200,000-gallon aquarium, an outdoor ski park and an arena for dolphin and killer whale shows that included alligators, sea lions, birds, shark-feeding, and snakes—crowned by kissing a cobra's flattened head. As the facilities deteriorated and splashier sea worlds opened, Sea Arama closed in 1990 and the last of its original buildings was torn down in 2006.

Sea Arama: 91st and Seawall
—Courtesy of The Rosenberg Library,
Galveston, Texas

6800 Seawall Boulevard

After you pass the light at 69th Street, you will note a Walmart below Seawall Boulevard on the left. This land witnessed one of the most heart-wrenching tragedies during Galveston's 1900 Storm.

The Sisters of Charity of the Incarnate Word cared for the children orphaned by the city's 1867 Yellow Fever epidemic. To house them, Bishop Claud Dubois bought Farnifala and Laura Green's house on this site in 1874, renaming it the St. Mary's Orphan Asylum. After one of its dormitories was damaged during a hurricane in 1876, a new boys' dorm was built three years later, but the orphanage did not receive its official Texas charter until twenty years later. To calm their fears as the winds of the storm howled and the rushing waters rose higher and higher, the nuns told the orphans to sing a simple French hymn, "Queen of the Waves"; meanwhile, in an effort to save all, each sister tied eight to ten children to her waist using clothesline. After the storm, the bodies of 90 children were found still tied to the nuns. The only survivors were three older boys who spent the night out in the open, clinging to the same tree.

▶ ❷ Pass Kroger and turn left at the light on 57th Street.

On the right stands the **Galveston Island Convention Center** which opened on May 6, 2004.

Lakeview Cemetery

On the west side of 57th Street, Lakeview Cemetery, the city's second oldest, was granted a charter by the state on July 5, 1886. A large granite "Grecian" sculpture designed by Pampeo Coppini of Florence, Italy, rises eight feet above the ground in a commanding position. Unveiled with much pomp and circumstance on May 21, 1905, the Galveston Tidal Wave Monument honors Joseph C. Root, founder of the Woodmen of the World, a fraternal organization and insurance company in Omaha, Nebraska.

Lakeview was also the final resting place for many Galveston notables, among them Walter Gresham, a Texas legislator and builder of the Bishop's Palace at 14th and Broadway, as well as prolific Prussian architect Alfred Muller. Post Civil War black activist, Norris Wright Cuney who died in March 1898, is buried near his daughter, Maud Hare. The grave of the first artistic director of the Little Theatre of Galveston, Peter Ames

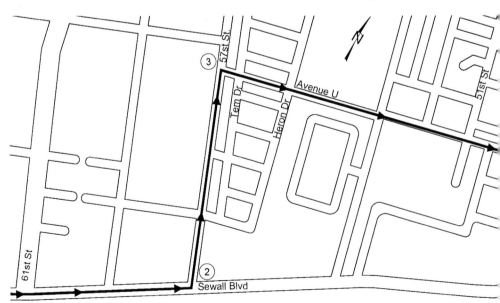

Lakeview Cemetery, 57th and Ave U

Vincent is marked by a simple headstone inscribed "Genius Walked Among Us" on the cemetery's north side. Perhaps the most famous man buried here is David G. Burnet, the provin-

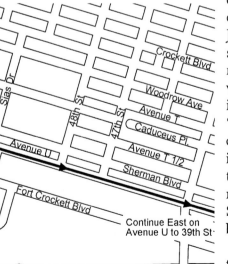

cial President of the Republic of Texas during the decisive Battle of San Jacinto, fought on April 21, 1836. He shares the second most prominent marker with Sidney Sherman, a colonel who fought in that battle, who is credited with creating the battle cry, "Remember the Alamo!" Burnet died on December 5, 1870, and was buried in the Magnolia Cemetery. In 1894 the Daughters of the Texas Revolution moved his remains to Lakeview beside Sherman's and erected a monument to both.

Reserved for the indigent and black, the New Potter's Field replaced the Old among the Broadway Cemeteries, moving to 59th and Avenue T½ during the early twentieth century.

This cemetery also served one man as his not-so-final resting place. French-born actor and playwright Charles Coghlan (1842-1899) gained fame on Dublin stages to secure passage across the Atlantic to the bright lights of Broadway. In 1876 he debuted at the Fifth Avenue Theatre. Acting alongside Fanny Davenport and Lilly Langtree, his career crested twenty-two years later when he starred in *The Royal Box*, his own adaptation of a Dumas play. "On the road" with it in Texas, he fell ill in Galveston and died at the Tremont House on November 27, 1899. His remains were placed in a metal casket and stored in a vault at Lakeview Cemetery, awaiting burial at his Prince Edward Island summer home. Somehow forgotten, they were swept out to sea during the 1900 Storm to be discovered seven years later just nine miles from the Island. However in 1927, the original story-spinners at *Ripley's Believe It or Not* reported that Coghlan's remains had really floated 2,000 miles on the Gulf Stream to their final resting place in Canada. This "Coffin Came Home" legend persists today.

▶ ❸ **Turn right on Avenue U; continue east to 39th Street.**

This city street marked the northern boundary of Fort Crockett, a U.S. military installation primarily used for basic and artillery training as well as a German prisoner of war camp. But the fort's history began way before that . . .

In 1897, the federal government purchased 125 acres of land from 45th to 49th streets on the beach to establish a military encampment for coastal defense along the southwestern Gulf of Mexico. Three concrete gun and mortar batteries were built before the federal government expanded the reservation to 53rd Street in April 1900. Plans to construct 18 buildings to house the 129 men of Battery C First Artillery base were underway when the 1900 Storm struck the Island on September 8, killing 29 soldiers; fortunately, the "guns and mortars suffered but slightly."

Three years later, the Fort Crockett Military Reservation was officially named after Tennessee pioneer hero Davy Crockett,

Fort Crockett, 53rd and Avenue U
—From the author's collection

who had fought and died defending the Alamo in 1836. The federal government extended the Seawall to 53rd Street in 1905 and six years later, 30 fire-proof, reinforced concrete buildings housed the Coast Artillery Corps. Those structures included several barracks, mess hall, hospital, administration building, post exchange and gymnasium (see the walking guide), completed just in time to serve as a mobilization center during the Mexican border war the following year.

During World War I, 100-200 dough boys went through basic training here per month before being deployed to France as replacements in the trenches, railroad artillery and Howitzer organizations.

During the second "war to end all wars," a total of 650 German POWs were detained between 57th and 53rd streets on Avenue U to the Seawall behind barb-wired fences with armed guards beginning in 1943; that same year secret fortifications were completed to protect against U-Boat attacks in the Gulf of Mexico. Although they proved unnecessary due to its shallow waters, Fort Crockett provided the Third Attack Group with artillery training at Battery Hoskins.

Fort Crocket German POW camp, 1943-45
—Courtesy of NOAA via sisters Ginger Forbs and
Nancy House whose father, Sgt. Rudolph Farmer,
guarded the prisoners

Deactivated in 1946, the grounds served as an R&R center for the Fourth Army, featuring fishing, bowling, tennis, archery, golf, horseback riding, and dancing until 1951, when it was declared surplus and released to the General Services Administration for disposal five years later.

The U.S. Fish and Wildlife Service acquired ten buildings the following year, which were transferred to the National Marine Fisheries Service of the Department of Commerce in 1970. That agency renovated six of the original buildings to house the National Oceanic and Atmospheric Administration Fisheries Service and Flower Garden Banks Marine Sanctuary. Today, NOAA's laboratory oversees commercial and recreational fishing, the ecology of coastal habitats and protection of endangered species of the Gulf and U.S. Caribbean.

Originally part of Fort Crocket, note the duplexes for the non-commissioned officers between 45th and 39th streets on your right, built in 1939. You will find more information about Fort Crockett, as well as the Denver Court development on the left, in the walking guide.

Crockett Court, 42nd and Avenue U
—From the author's collection

Crockett Court

On May 18, 1937, the Crockett Courts opened 21 individual brick veneer cottages with an office and commissary to meet the modest needs of families of "the premier resort of the Southwest, Galveston Island." Adjoining the Fort Crockett military installation on Avenue U, the tourist camp was reported to be water- and insect-proof for year-round comfort. Designed by R. R. Rapp, the "homey" eight large and thirteen efficiency tourist cottages were built by J. A. Torregrossa

▶ ❹ Turn left on 39th Street.

To your right, you'll pass the west side of Gaido's Seafood Restaurant with its private Pelican Club in back. Marked on the Seawall by its landmark extra jumbo fiberglass crab, "caught in Galveston Bay," it opened in 1911 on Murdock's Pier over the Gulf at 23rd Street. Its fourth-generation Italian immigrant owners have built a nationwide reputation for the freshest and most consistent seafood dishes.

Gaido's on Murdock's Pier, 22nd and Seawall
—From the author's collection

▶ **Continue driving north.**

Galveston College

In September 1967 this two-year junior college opened in Moody Hall, a rehabilitated orphanage at the corner of 42nd and Avenue Q, surrounded by a middle-class residential neighborhood. With its two-fold focus on low-cost freshman/sophomore basic courses and medical occupational studies in conjunction with the University of Texas Medical Branch, this junior college had expanded with new buildings south to Avenue R by 1976. It opened its Fort Crockett campus at 50th and Avenue U (see the walking guide) the following year, to include criminal justice studies and the Upper Deck Theatre. With the addition of culinary arts and hospitality, GC consolidated back to its Avenue Q roots in 2004, spreading eastward to 38th Street with its new Beacon Square entrance and parking lots.

▶ ❺ **Turn right on Avenue P½. Park in front of the first house listed and walk the next two blocks.**

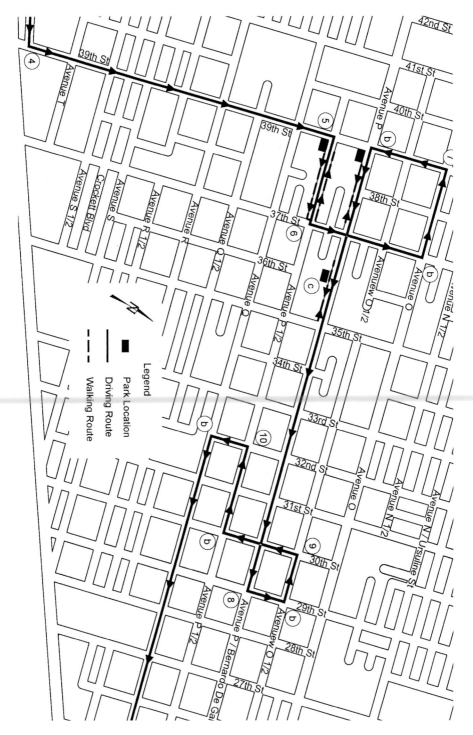

3823 Avenue P½

The property between 37th and 38th streets was part of Thomas H. Borden's outlot; the 1845 Sandusky map shows a windmill Borden had built here. During the early "Roarin' Twenties," it was developed as the city's first residential neighborhood with deed restrictions—perfect for Galveston's elite of the era! The new architect in town, Raymond R. Rapp, designed most of the homes in this Nichols-Byrne subdivision. Built in 1924 for Dr. William F. Spiller, this quaint stuccoed cottage featured a screened-in front porch.

3828 Avenue P½

On the north side of the street, Rapp designed this house for Edward Rudge Allen in 1923 . . .

3806 Avenue P½

. . . as well as this home for Charles A. Holtone one year later. Across the street, note the 1926 raised craftsman cottage at **3805.**

3724 Avenue P½

"BOI" on October 11, 1884, Alexander Baptiste Shoomer worked his way up in the steamship business to become Vice President of S. Sgitcovich, Agents and Brokers, during the 1930s. In 1924, he hired local contractor Ernest Babb to build this Craftsman bungalow, probably from a contractor's pattern book, for his wife and son. Typical of the style are the large windows, small wrap-around front porch supported by brick piers, and a number of interior built-ins. When his wife died three years later, he married May Flanagan, who bore him two daughters. They moved to Houston in 1944 and Shoomer sold the home to Mitchell and Uryth Morrissey.

1919 37th Street

John Settles bought this land in 1896 and commissioned Nicholas J. Clayton to design this delightful Queen Ann home. Note its large wraparound veranda and balconette in the front gable. After the home was completed three years later, a mysterious Miss Ida B. Baden, who had extensive real estate holdings and owned stock in the Galveston Wharf Company, paid him in

1919
37th
Street

cash for the property. Unfortunately, she died suddenly at age 43 in 1906, leaving an estate valued at $50,000 to her sister in Boston. Benno Sproule, the owner of a freight brokerage business, bought the house in 1913. His widow, who became one of American National Insurance Company's most successful underwriters, continued to live here after his death in 1932 with her five daughters. After she sold the home in 1959, it changed hands several times until it was sold and restored in 1975.

▶ **6** Back in your car, turn left on 37th Street, then turn left again on the one-way Avenue O.

3701 Avenue O

Carmelo LaBarbera built his corner grocery store in 1906. It still has a canopy over its street sidewalks. Across 37th Street on the southeast corner was the West End Bakery, built two years later in a classic wooden square. In an area full of "fixer-uppers," think of the potential!

3827 Avenue O

3827 Avenue O

John Sealy founded the Magnolia Petroleum Company (named for his aunt who lived at 25th and Broadway in Open Gates) together with his brother-in-law R. Waverly Smith. One of its oldest surviving brick gas stations, built in 1926, stands on this corner.

▶ **7 Turn left on 39th Street and left again at the stop light on Bernardo de Galvez (aka Avenue P), a one-way street going east (note that both names are used in this guide).**

This street—as well as the city, island and surrounding Bay—was named for the Spanish viceroy who first commissioned a survey of the island and its bay in 1784. At the age of 40 two years later in New Orleans, the Count died of Yellow Fever and never stepped foot in "Galvez Town" (later shortened to Galveston). Park and walk the next block, but first read the historical marker facing 39th Street in honor of **Thomas Henry Borden.**

3827 Avenue P

Born in Norwich, New York on January 28, 1804, he joined

Stephen F. Austin's "Old Three Hundred" in 1824. His older brother Gail followed him to Texas five years later and succeeded him as Austin's official surveyor. While Thomas helped lay out both cities of Galveston and Houston before the state's War for Independence from Mexico, his brother sold 2,500 lots for the Galveston City Company. The older Borden found his calling as an inventor and moved to New York in 1856 to patent his process for condensed milk.

Even though Thomas owned much land in Fort Bend and Brazoria counties, the younger Borden brother chose to stay on Galveston Island to farm. Also bitten by the invention bug, he invented a gauge for steam boats, built the first windmill on his property and some even think he fashioned the terraqueous machine that traveled on both land and sea, which is often attributed to Gail. Unfortunately however, not believing in the power of patents, Thomas Henry Borden died rather destitute in his adopted city on March 16, 1877. His house was built three years earlier and lacked much of the more ornate Victorian features which reflected his lack of wealth.

Arts and Crafts Cottages

Another popular architectural style found scattered throughout several Galveston neighborhoods is the quaint Arts and Crafts cottage. Built as early as 1907 in the East End historic districts, this popular middle-class floor plan spread west during the 1920s–1940s. In recent years, owners have started restoring these craftsman bungalows, sprinkled few and far between in the large Kempner Park and Lasker neighborhoods. As you drive the long and circuitous route, note the potential for further rebirth by restoration of this genre.

3823 Avenue P

Addison V. Purdy, owner of a book store on Market, built this classic Arts and Crafts cottage, with its large front porch and porte-cochere, during the spring of 1923. He lived here with his son Paul and daughter-in-law Bernice until 1945, when Pauline Burney bought the house. She added an extra front door to accommodate her one-room beauty parlor. Several years later, she married Kurt Teager, brewmaster at the Falstaff

3823 Ave P (aka Bernardo de Galvez Ave)

Brewery. In 1975, the bungalow sold to a young married couple, Don and Francis Howell, who lived here for thirty years.

3815 Bernardo de Galvez

Next door, almost hidden behind an iron fence and trees, stands a 1928 French Country home, designed by Houston architect John Staub. Built for cotton exporter William C. Helmbrecht, the rather austere orange, black and yellow brick house featured two small oval windows on either side of the front door with louvered blinds surrounding both door and windows.

3812 Avenue P

Self-taught engineer, builder and house mover John Egert, born in Frankfurt, Germany, was instrumental in the post-1900 Storm clean-up of the Island. In 1905 he had originally built this ornate Victorian home at 2319 37th Street. Ten years later Egert updated his Victorian by adding a Craftsman porch. The Galveston Historical Foundation rescued it from demolition in early 1985 and moved it seven blocks to this site across Avenue P in March of the following year. Its restoration complete, it was featured on the annual Homes Tour in May 1987.

▶ Retrace your steps back to your car. Now driving, cross 37th Street and park your car in front of the Samuel May Williams house.

Walk east on the south side of the street to 35th Street for a more up-close-and-personal look. This is one of those areas with no sidewalks, so please watch your step!

3601 Bernardo de Galvez

According to a popular legend, this simple New England planter's house was prefabricated in Maine and shipped by schooner in 1839. When it landed on Galveston Island, Samuel May Williams was out-of-town—again—on the state's business. So he asked his business partner, Thomas McKinney, to supervise the building of both their houses on rural outlots about two miles west of the city's central business district. Facing it east to catch the southern breezes, the house was erected on 10-foot pilings on this section of William's twenty acres. From the cupola, the banker, who had served as Stephen F. Austin's chief

3600 Ave P

financial officer during Texas' war of independence, could scan the beach or watch his business at his port. However, it seemed as though he came "home only long enough to father the next child," leaving wife Sara to raise their ten children she bore him as well as another son, Joseph Guadalupe Victoria Williams, whose mother Sam had banished so that he could marry a younger and more respectable woman. Unfortunately, only seven lived to adulthood.

After his death in 1858, Sarah remained here until her death two years later. The house was sold to the Philip C. Tucker family, who owned it until 1954, when the Galveston Historical Foundation bought and restored the house. No longer open as a museum, the Samuel May Williams home now serves as a private residence.

3523 Avenue P

Amid post 1957 construction on both sides of the street, notice the peaked roof and decorative gingerbread of this cottage. Designed by C. W. Bulger in 1896, this house was built for James W. Foster of the Gulf, Colorado and Santa Fe Railroad.

3503—at the corner of 35th and Avenue P

Dr. Frederick K. Fisher, the State Quarantine officer for Indianola since 1877, moved to Galveston Island after that city was destroyed in the 1886 hurricane. In addition to his quarantine duties here, he also served as a physician and surgeon at St. Mary's Hospital. Built two years later for his wife Addy, this quaint 1888 Victorian stick house features fish scale siding and elaborate gingerbread over its small wraparound porch. Although the Fishers had no children of their own, they raised nephew, F. Kenner Fisher, who had been orphaned during the 1900 Storm. When he died in 1912 age 11, they donated land to St. Mary's Orphanage for a park in his memory.

▶ **Cross Avenue P and turn left, retracing your steps west.**

3502 Bernardo de Galvez

Directly across the street stands a stately American Neoclassical. UTMB Professor of Medicine Dr. and Mrs. Edward

35th and Ave P, Randall Home

Randall, Jr., had originally hired Houston architect John F. Staub to restore the dilapidated 1859 Southern townhouse built for Mary Williams and Thomas J. League. Since no contractor would bid on it, the architect designed this minimalist modern red brick house in 1929. He added the east wing three years later and the west, in 1936. Obscured by a tree-covered iron fence with its spacious front lawn full of live oaks and magnolias, Staub recreated the Ave O Villa District (see the walking guide) on Ave P for this grandson of William P. Ballinger.

3528 Bernardo de Galvez

Samuel May Williams' grandson, Thomas J. League, Jr., built this solidly centered square house in 1893, just down the street from his parents. Brick piers replaced the original veranda supports just after the 1900 Storm.

3602 Bernardo de Galvez

Two doors down stands the Samuel Campbell home built as a one-story in 1887. Somewhat of a mystery house, that original

single story home was raised and a new 1st floor built beneath.
Note its stained and leaded glass windows for what now serves
as a bed and breakfast.

▶ **Finding yourself back at your car, continue driving east on
this one-way street.**

3421 Avenue P

Wholesale grocer, Louis R. Koester built this raised Victorian
cottage in 1898 as rental property. Note its decorative screen-
ing on the front porch. The house at **3327** was built in 1915.

34th and Bernardo de Galvez

Standing at the curb on the left-hand side of the street just to
the left of a house marked **3410**, you will find a grey granite
Texas Centennial monument installed in 1936 to mark the site
of Gail Borden's home from 1837–1851.

3201 Avenue P

This 1892 raised cottage was built by Swedish-born stevedore
Charles T. Suderman. His business partner, Ben Dolson, Jr.,
lived next door.

3121, 3115 and 3101 Avenue P

Three doctors chose this block to build their homes in the early
1920s. The first two larger houses belonged to Dr. Julius L.
Jinkins and Dr. Edward M. F. Stephens, respectively. Dr. Cooper
P. Bevil owned the third, a stucco bungalow trimmed with dark
red brick.

3011 Avenue P

Walter H. Laycock, chief clerk for wholesale grocers and ship
handlers H. Mosle & Company, hired C. W. Bulger to build this
decorative Victorian in 1898. Note the elements of Queen Anne
in its front porch on its east side and fancy gabled entry. On the
north side of the Street, **3012 Avenue P** was built in 1891.

3007 Avenue P

Note the double gallery of this house, built the same year as
Laycock's, across the avenue.

2927 Avenue P

Standing behind a black-&-red tiled sidewalk, so typical of the East End in the 1880s, this house was probably built around then but was expanded several times after the 1900 Storm. It is estimated that owner and builder, James K. Deats, added the gabled entry, carried by coupled columns, five years later.

2928 Avenue P

Across the avenue, Robbie and Benjamin C. Doherty built their modest raised cottage in 1907, with a large wrap-around porch on its west side. Its front elevation featured a gabled bay to the east of its center hall plan. Owner of a clothing store on Market, they lived here until 1920. The house was sold after a series of owners to Federal Judge Hugh Gibson and his wife Evelyn in 1954, who continued to live here until 1998. After being restored in 2005, the current owners then had to redesign the first floor in 2010 due to damage caused during Hurricane Ike.

▶ **❽ Turn left on 29th Street, then left again on Avenue O½.**

29th and Ave O½

2902 Avenue O½

This 20' x 14' Victorian cottage once adjoined the 1858 Greek Revival mansion of Texas' first lawyer, William Pitt Ballinger, as his home office and library. Crowned "The Cradle," it witnessed the foundation of the Daughters of the Republic of Texas by his middle daughter Betty with her cousin Hally Bryan on November 6, 1891. Dedicated to preserve the history of the state's republic, membership in the organization was open only to those women who were "all lineal descendants of the heroes of the Texas Revolution." Located on the northwest corner of 29th and Avenue O on a ten-acre outlot called "The Oaks," the Ballinger home was destroyed during the Great Storm of 1900 save for its library, which was sold and moved. The library with its 12-foot ceilings and bay window on its east side was not found until 1937, two blocks south between Avenues N and N½ when it was moved and rebuilt at Menard Park, near 29th and Avenue Q. The Ballingers donated this corner in 1973, and "The Cradle" was returned to within a block of its original location. Its final dedication happened on April 8, 1975, in memory of Mrs. Libby Shearn Moody.

▶ **❾ Turn left on 30th Street and right on Avenue P½.**

3102 Avenue P½

Built in 1895 for feed, grain and fertilizer dealer Charles W. Eisenfelder, this raised Gulf Coast cottage featured a window bay within its wrap-around veranda, unroofed on its east side, and two dormers.

3127 Avenue P½

On the other end and side of the block stands the 1909 Albert A. Fedder home. A maker of metal building parts, he fashioned an unusual, geometric roof design from his products atop a broad front entry. While it was being built, it appears he lived in the raised house around the corner at **2010 32nd Street**.

3202 Avenue P½

This raised and dormered Victorian, built in 1892, tips its hat toward those in the East End with its elaborate "spindle-and-ball" gingerbread on its porches.

▶ ⑩ Turn left on 32nd Street, then left again on Avenue Q. Drive east until you get to Rosenberg Avenue (aka 25th Street).

3202 Avenue Q

On the corner to your left, note this two-story Craftsman built by contractor Hart H. Settle around 1912, located in the Fort Crocket neighborhood. Typical of the architectural style are exposed rafters and wide wrap-around front porch supported by squared columns.

3101 Avenue Q

German carpenter Christian L. Wolfer built this quaint 1891 Victorian front-gabled, raised cottage. After it suffered extensive damage during Hurricane Ike, its owners donated the house to the Galveston Historical Foundation, which moved it to this location, 17 blocks away from its original. Nicknamed the Green Revival House, the cottage was restored as part of the new historic preservation movement sweeping across the nation. Certified Platinum by the United States Green Building Council for its Leadership in Energy and Environmental Design, the Foundation has garnered much national recognition for their efforts. On the same side of the avenue, note the cute cottage at **3109**, built in 1955.

2012 29th Street

Two blocks further east, you will pass the back of Menard Park on your right-hand side, with its modern skateboard park and tennis courts. Next door fronting 27th Street, a former World War II USO became a city-run recreation building until its roof collapsed in 2004 and it had to be demolished. Two years later, Parks and Recreation announced plans to update the park.

On the Seawall, the Jessie McGuire Dent Recreation Center opened Spring 2009, named after Central High School's Latin teacher and Dean of Girls. In 1943, she had also advocated for and won equal pay for all Texas teachers regardless of color. Her father was Robert Maguire, an African American hack stand operator who owned the land between 29th and 27th streets on the beach. His two blocks became the entertainment venue for the city's black community, hosting many Juneteenth and other family celebrations. The beach across what would become the Seawall was strictly open only for "people of color." However, after the grade raising, all that "land was later taken from them," according to Izola Collins in her book *Island of Color*. In 1914, the city developed Menard Park and playground and, as they say, the rest is history.

▶ You will complete your drive of historic Galveston to the eastern end of the Island in the next and final chapter.

Galveston's Original Pleasure Pier 25th and Seawall
—From the author's collection

CHAPTER 9

All the Way East!

▶ ❶ **From Avenue Q where Chapter 8 ended, turn left on Rosenberg Avenue.**

Just before you turn north on 25th Street, glance to your right to see the newly-restored Pleasure Pier. Originally built in 1944 by the Maceos, it was air conditioned by W. L. Moody four years later—just in time to host Mardi Gras King Charlie McCarthy with his voice, Edgar Bergen. (For more information, please refer to *Walking Historic Galveston: A Guide to its Neighborhoods*)

2018-24 Rosenberg

Built by Mrs. Eva Dorfman and Miss Sadell Dorfman in 1939, the modern, brick Waldorf Apartments with their flat roof sharply contrast with the Victorian and Queen Anne designs further north on the avenue. Also note how their design optimizes the southern sea breeze off the Gulf.

2002 Rosenberg

One block further, this cluster of almost identical two-story houses, built in 1913 by Mr. and Mrs. W. G. Tabb, continues around the corner of Avenue P½ to 24th Street.

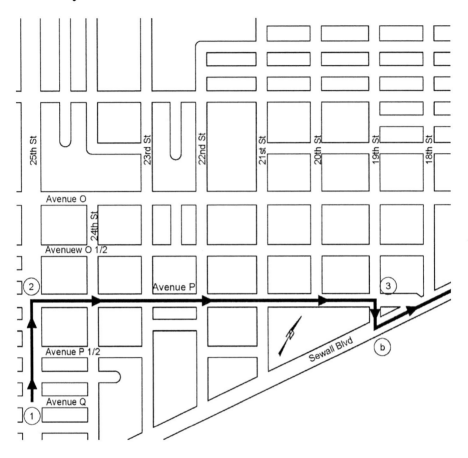

1917 Rosenberg

Across the avenue, the round entry bay of this 1925 Mediterranean is truly a one-of-a-kind on Galveston Island. Built by Max Baum, who owned a loan company, its red-tiled roof also distinguishes this stuccoed two-story.

Replaced by a grocery store in 1966, an elementary school once stood at the corner of 25th Street and Avenue P. Designed by Nicholas Clayton in 1893, it opened as Bath Avenue Elementary, so named after the city's primary north/south corridor. Heavily damaged during the 1900 Storm, it was finally repaired in 1908 and reopened the following June. Since Bath Avenue had been renamed Rosenberg Avenue in April 1900 to honor Galveston's most generous benefactor Henry Rosenberg, the school was renamed Sam Houston Elementary in 1914. Closed in 1965, the historic Clayton building was demolished.

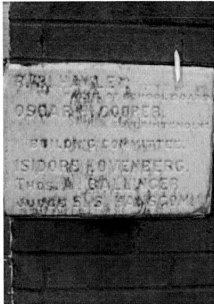

Front and side view of the elementary school, 25th and Ave P

The school's original white marble cornerstone noting Bath Avenue School has been salvaged and placed under the guardianship of the Galveston Historical Foundation.

▶ ❷ Turn right onto the one-way Avenue P, aka Bernardo de Galvez

Bernardo de Galvez was a Spanish count who commissioned a survey of the Island, its natural harbor and surrounding bay in 1746 and for whom it is named. He died in New Orleans of Yellow Fever two years later, never having visited the area.

2408 and 2406 Avenue P

Building contractor J. W. Zempter constructed these two tenant cottages in 1910. From the first, one had an excellent view of the Letitia Rosenberg Home for Women (see the walking guide for further information). He lived around the corner at **1813 24th Street**.

▶ Continue driving east three blocks.

2102 Avenue P

At the corner of 21st and P stands a high-raised cottage, built by the grandson of Prussian immigrant, Nicholas Gengler. Joseph L. hired the company of Ullman, Lewis and Co. to construct the house, complete with cistern, stable and chicken coop, in 1905. Note its gabled front on the west side of the porch, which wraps around its east side, strategically placed to catch the Gulf's southern breezes. Although president of a successful grocery store on Market founded by his father and uncle in 1851, he and his brother Charles moved to San Antonio around 1915 for health reasons and perhaps to found a chain of stores all their own.

Looking catty-cornered at the intersection, note the west side entrance of the Hotel Galvez, topped by the head of a Spanish conquistador. This third entrance to the hotel now houses the new Spa.

Hotel Galvez

Between 21st and 19th Streets, you will drive past the rear entrance to the Hotel Galvez, built by a group of city businessmen in 1911 to symbolize Galveston's return as a beach resort after its recovery from the devastating 1900 Storm. Adorned by marble plaques with differing emblems, it was originally intended as the main entrance by St. Louis architects Mauran and Russell as this north-facing door featured a porte cochere complete with mission parapet. Centered within, you'll find Count Bernardo de Galvez's family coat of arms, with its motto: "Yo Solo" or "I Alone." Probably due to the grandeur of its expansive lawn, Gulf view and courtyard, the main entrance switched to the south side of the hotel. Through the years, it was this famous image that adorned postcards, sales collateral and many photographs. You will find MUCH more information about Galveston's "million dollar monument" in the walking guide.

1918 Avenue P

Behind the hotel but still enjoying a delightful view of the Gulf with its southern breezes, this house is distinguished by its unique color scheme. Perhaps it was a product of GHF's Paint Partnership program for low-income home owners wherein they do the painting and the Foundation supplies the paint—in approved actual Victorian color combinations.

▶ ❸ **Turn right on 19th Street, then left on Seawall Boulevard.**

Your leisurely driving tour of historic Galveston continues by travelling east on the Seawall, which means TRAFFIC, especially during the spring and summer months! For safety's sake, please read the background information before driving to where the Gulf of Mexico meets the Bay, providing a passageway to Houston's Ship Channel.

Rear entrance of Hotel Galvez, 21st and Ave P

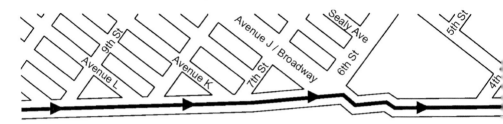

The Seawall's Beginnings

The first section of a solid concrete breakwater, nicknamed the Seawall, was completed on July 29, 1904. Financed by the County, its construction began near the Bay at 8th, then turned south at 6th Street to the beachfront. Stretching westward to 23rd Street, a pair of concrete monuments still marks its completion, as well as the completion of the Grade Raising to this point in 1911.

Note the granite rock groins stretching into the water at various intervals; they were added to the original Seawall in 1936 to prevent the sand from washing from beneath the concrete breakwater (for further information about the building of the Seawall, see Chapter 5 of the walking guide).

Seawall, Concrete Mixer (Corps of Engineers)
—From the author's collection

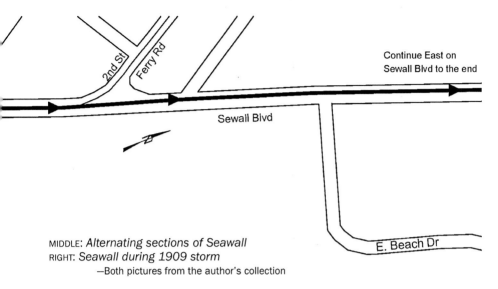

Continue East on
Sewall Blvd to the end

Sewall Blvd

2nd St

Ferry Rd

E. Beach Dr

MIDDLE: *Alternating sections of Seawall*
RIGHT: *Seawall during 1909 storm*
 —Both pictures from the author's collection

1802 Seawall

The last remaining private residence on the Seawall, this simple stucco house with its arched verandas was built in 1913 by Fred A. Langbehn. Also designed by the shipping agent, its deep pilings and reinforced concrete walls protected it from the fuller force of a hurricane in 1915.

The structures you'll pass on the left are mostly tourist-related retail outlets, fast-food drive-thru's, souvenir shops, restaurants, hotels and motels which are far less than historical.

On the mostly empty lot at 8th Street once stood the cruise ship-shaped S.S. Galveston Motel/Courts. Ben Milam designed his nautical modernistic hotel to fit an oddly-shaped lot for local restaurateurs, the Hill brothers in 1941. It was razed in 2006 to make way for a high rise condominium which has yet to be built.

On the sand to your right, you will pass several public beach parks befitting a popular resort town. The largest and best known is Stewart Beach accessed by its ramp at 6th Street that leads to its pavilion.

Where the Emerald condominiums now stand at the corner of 6th and Seawall Boulevard, the Jack Tar Court-Hotel once stretched to Holiday Drive, across the street from East Beach — "at the Southern end of the U.S. Highway 75." Originally constructed in 1940, twelve two-story buildings housed private one, two and three room studio apartments, complete with kitchenettes—65 in all, designed by Thomas Price. The property featured a palm-lined figure-8 swimming pool, a private club named the Quarter Deck and the Coffee Cove, offering "Ship-Shape Services" on its large, distinctive neon sign. Thirteen years later, an expansion added a multi-level resort area complete with water fall and picturesque bridge over the pool. Reopening in July 1954, it was "THE" place to be during the 1960s! Twenty years later, however, the Jack Tar had fallen into vagrant-laden disrepair, condemned then demolished in 1988.

After you pass the traffic light at Holiday Drive, continue driving east on the Seawall. The next intersection leads to Ferry Road, veering off to the left. This leads to a free ride across Galveston Bay to Bolivar Peninsula, run by the Texas

Jack Tar Court-Hotel, 6th and Seawall 1941
—From the author's collection

Department of Transportation. This year-round, 24/7 operation makes the 2½-mile trip every 20 minutes from 6 AM to midnight, using as many as five vessels at peak times; the grave-yard schedule runs every hour. For a cool water wildlife adventure with someone else driving, take the time to enjoy this windy ride on the ferry, followed by flocks of laughing gulls looking for a snack and sometimes featuring entertainment by wild dolphins! You can park your car and walk aboard the ferry at one of its two landings, guarded by pelicans. If you choose to drive onto the ferry, remember that you must drive off and wait in traffic on the Port Bolivar side before you re-board the vessel for the return trip.

Across from the intersection of Seawall and Ferry Road now stands an upscale RV Park and Resort on the sand.

The Building of the Eastern Extension of the Seawall

In 1913, a special board of engineers recommended that the concrete breakwater be extended to the South Jetty a total of 12,000 feet to protect the federal battery at Fort San Jacinto. Three years later, the United States Congress authorized the project, even though work did not begin until 1918. An additional 10-foot embankment behind the bulwark separated the Seawall from the quicksand-dotted marsh, perhaps a result of the Grade Raising. Twice lack of funds interrupted the extension, under the supervision of Thomas W. Forman, so the double-decker breakwater was not completed until December 4, 1925. High school students on the Island will fondly remember that second concrete embankment as "Cherry Hill,"—a good place to "park . . ."

To the right, you will notice several new and newer condominiums on the beach. Moving west to east, they include the condominiums By the Sea, the double Palisade Palms and the Galvestonian. The newest addition is called Beachtown—a sandy subdivision that features million-dollar high-raised residences, modern but with a nod to Victorian architecture.

The drive following the Seawall to its end at Boddeker Drive is worth the view. Both entering and leaving Galveston Bay are huge cargo ships en route to or from the Houston Ship Channel, which was not constructed until 1914. If you're lucky enough to see a cruise ship on the horizon, know that their safe harbor is the Port of Galveston. Park your car facing north and step out to enjoy the quiet lapping of the Gulf against the jetty. A placard sitting next to an observation point of Fort San Jacinto Point chronicles its history with maps, historical images and a time line. Also noted is a number of species of shorebirds that winter at Big Reef or Apffel Park, including various gulls and plovers, American oystercatchers, egrets, herons and Rosette spoonbills.

For a more up close and personal natural experience, turn southward to drive through the dunes and flocks of sea birds along Boddeker Drive. Practically eye-to-eye with the sea, notice the fishermen, both male and female, on both sides, sometimes with just their heads sticking above the water. There is a city beach park at the very end that charges for parking on its sand, but there is a "Free Parking" spot to the left. Take care, however, so that your car does not get stuck in the beach's shifting sands!

From (almost) one end of the Island to the other in three chapters, your drive *Beyond the Beaten Paths* is now complete!

Bibliography

"A Riding and Walking Tour of a Residential Community Listed in the National Register of Historic Places." East End Historical District Association. Various n.d. revisions.

Barnstone, Howard. *The Galveston That Was*. Houston: Rice University Press, 1966, 1993.

Beasley, Ellen and Stephen Fox. *Galveston Architecture Guidebook*. Houston: Rice University Press, 1996.

Briscoe Center for American History website.

Cartwright, Gary. *Galveston: A History of the Island*. New York: Atheneum, Macmillan Publishing Company, 1991.

———. *Hotel Galvez: Queen of the Gulf*. Galveston: Mitchell Historic Properties, 2010.

Chance, Jane. Application to the Texas Historical Commission for an Official Texas Historic Landmark Plaque for the John Davidson-Samuel Moore Penland House, 1207 Postoffice, n.p. 2010.

City of Galveston Historic Districts. Galveston: Department of Planning and Community Development. n.p., 2002.

Clark, Kirk. Personal notes on the Nottingham Lace Factory, August 9, 2012.

Davis, Albert B., Jr. *Galveston's Bulwark Against the Sea: History of the Galveston Sea Wall*. U.S. Corps of Engineers. Presentation made at the Second Annual Conference on Coastal Engineering, 1951.

Davis, Brian M. *Images of America: Lost Galveston*. Charleston, SC: Arcadia Publishing, 2010.

Eisenhour, Virginia. *Galveston: A Different Place*. Published by the Author, 1986.

Find-A-Grave website.

Galveston Daily News. Various articles, 1841–2012.

Galveston Historic Homes Tour brochures. Galveston Historical Foundation. n.p., 1974-2012.

Henson, Margaret Sweet. *Samuel May Williams: Early Texas Entrepreneur*. Published by the Author, 1976.

Hotel Galvez: Queen of the Gulf. Galveston, Mitchell Historic Properties, 2010.

Houston Association of Realtors, Multiple Listing Services Online.

Hyman, Harold M. *Oleander Odyssey: The Kempners of Galveston, Texas, 1854–1980s*. College Station: Texas A&M University Press, 1990.

JeanLafitte.net website.

Leavenworth, Geoffrey. *Historic Galveston*. Houston: Herring Press, 1985.

Lienhard, John H. "The Engines of Our Ingenuity: Episode 1099: Robert's Rules of Order." Houston: University of Houston, KUHF Radio, 1996.

McComb, David G. *Galveston: A History*. Austin: University of Texas Press, 1986.

Miller, Ray. *Ray Miller's Galveston*. Austin: Capital Printing, 1983.

National Oceanic and Atmospheric Administration. *History of Fort Crockett, Galveston, Texas*. Compiled by Jo Anne Williams: various materials including CD, timeline, images, newspaper articles, and maps.

National Register of Historic Places Online. Washington, D.C.: National Park Service. http://www.nps.gov/history/nr.

Nesbitt, Bob. *Bob's Reader*, 1985 Edition. Self-published.

Newspaper Archives through the Rosenberg Library website.

"Old Red: Ashbel Smith Building." *Galveston: The University of Texas Medical Branch*. 1988. Online Revisions.

Pinckard, Jane Burton, and Rebecca Sealy Pinckard. *Lest We Forget: The Open Gates*. Houston: Published by the Authors, 1988.

Rosenberg Library's Galveston and Texas History Center, 2310 Sealy, Galveston, TX 77550. Various archival, photos, and emphemera materials.

Sacred Places: Galveston's Historic Religious Institutions tour brochures, Volumnes II, VI, VII and 14th Annual. Galveston Historical Foundation. n.p.

Scardino, Barrie and Drexel Turner. *Clayton's Galveston: The Architecture of Nicholas J. Clayton and His Contemporaries*. College Station: Texas A&M University Press, 2000.

Schneider, Paul. *Brutal Journey: Cabeza de Vaca and the Epic First Crossing of North America*. New York, NY: Holt Paperback, 2007.

THC Atlas Online. Austin: Texas Historical Commission. http://atlas.thc.state .tx.us.

Texas State Historical Association. *Handbook of Texas Online*. http://www.tshaon line.org.

Wiencek, Henry. *The Moodys of Galveston and Their Mansion*. Galveston, TX: The Mary Moody Northen Endowment, 2010.

Wikipedia, "the free encyclopedia" online.

Wright-Gidley, Jodi and Jennifer Marines. *Galveston: A City on Stilts*. Charleston SC: Arcadia Publishing. 2008.

About the Author

Fifth generation "BOI" (aka Born on the Island), Jan Johnson has been seriously studying the rich history of Galveston as a part-time Tour Guide since 1982. A direct descendant of two 1900 Storm survivors, her interest in her Island heritage was born when her mother, Dorris Stechmann Johnson, became secretary to John Garner's Historic American Buildings Survey in 1966-67.

Jan earned a Bachelor of Science in Elementary Education at the University of Houston, Clear Lake, in 1986 with a 3.94 GPA. In 1995, she attained her Masters of Art in Literature from UHCL, researching and writing about Galveston's Little Theatre. Focused on writing her city's tour guide tales, she took the full time "free fall with free lancing" in May 2000, naming her "micro" company, "Galveston Island Gal."

The idea of writing a walking guide of the historic Island presented itself through Bed-&-Breakfast owners Jim and Sally Laney, circa 2002. After spending a week in Key West, Florida, with her Michigan cousins who lazed around the pool, she walked the western-most Key's historic streets using its various guidebooks. Returning home, she outlined her book and found a publisher two years later. She completed the manuscript, maps, and photos in September 2007. Despite her father's diagnosis of Alzheimer's, and switching publishers in mid-stream, followed by the devastation of Hurricane Ike which uprooted her from her historic birth city, *Walking Historic Galveston: A Guide to its Neighborhoods* appeared on bookshelves in March/April 2009.

The city's first practical, comprehensive walking guide offers walker-friendly routes of nine distinct districts, concentrated with structures from the past. Written in a very readable voice and offered at a nominal cost, the book is designed for the "Everyman" who wanders the streets and wonders about the inside human stories of those who lived, loved, and worked in the unusual buildings that survived them.

Jan's second book, *Beyond the Beaten Paths: Driving Historic Galveston*, begins where the first left off, with an ambitious goal of including all that was left out of the first. Readers travel the Island's streets from the port to the gulf, meandering in and out of the East End before walking two areas: one of the downtown "Arts and Entertainment" Postoffice District and the Broadway Cemetery. Driving west to the airport through middle-class neighborhoods, the driving guide leads you "Down the Island" to Jamaica Beach, then returns you via a circuitous route to the very eastern tip of the Seawall—from (almost) one end of the Island to the other—in three chapters! Along the way, happy wanderers encounter the usual colorful and somewhat infamous characters who pepper the Island's past, set among many vintage images.